So You Want to
BUILD a
HOUSE

Don Lohnes

ISBN

Hardcover: 978-1-967668-88-5
Paperback: 978-1-967668-87-8

Contents

Acknowledgements

I also wish to thank the following people for providing support and assistance during the writing, John Mogan of Halifax and Bob Mossman of Lunenburg, Nova Scotia, Canada for suggestions regarding language. Also, I wish to thank David Windau of Tiffin, Ohio, USA and Mario Vuotto of Halifax, Nova Scotia, Canada for their advice given for the section on financing. Furthermore, I would like to thank Sandy Rutledge, Andy Lynch, Scott Smith and Harold Daley all of Halifax, Nova Scotia, Canada for providing their endorsements.

Lastly, I wish to thank my wife Pam for her continued support from beginning to end.

Costs provided in this book are provided as a guide only as they increased since the original publication in 2014.

Dedication

*I dedicate this book to my lifelong friend, **John Douglas Dauphinee**, alias **Skipper**, who unfortunately passed away during its writing. We were childhood friends and continued to be through life until he passed during the spring of 2014. We both enjoyed building and shared many projects together helping each other throughout the process.*

Rest in peace; March 1st, 1946 – May 1st, 2014.

Endorsements

"An excellent source of information for anyone considering buying some property and building a house. Takes you through the necessary stages required in the process."

Scott Smith, *president Rooftight Homes Limited*

Fall River, Nova Scotia

"This little book has big advice to take you through the steps required in building a home. A very useful tool even if you are not building; but considering buying a home. Full of valuable information"

Sandy Rutledge, *FRI, Broker Domus Reality*

Halifax, Nova Scotia

"Finally someone has taken the time to put the elements of building a home in simple and concise language that anyone can understand. Full of real life examples of some of the pitfalls that can occur when taking on a project of this nature."

Andrew Lynch, *FRAIC*

Halifax, Nova Scotia

"If you are considering building a house, this book is a must to read. It takes you from the initial conception stage to the move in date in a language and logical progression. The process as described also works for the larger projects that our company deals with."

Harold Daley, *president Ashford Properties Ltd.*

Moncton, New Brunswick

Foreword

SO YOU WANT TO BUILD A HOUSE. For some time you have been thinking of building your own house. Well, go for it. It is not as difficult a task as you may think. However, there are many pitfalls that can arise and they can dampen your spirit. There are things to think about and sequences of construction that are important for a successful project. For example: Is this your first house? Do you plan to raise a family here? Do you plan to retire here? These are just some of the many questions that you must ask yourself. In the end you may not be the actual builder. You may contract out the various phases and control the project in that manner, or, you may just hire a contractor to build your dream house. Another option would be to buy a house that is already built. In all these cases this book will assist by providing you with some knowledge of what to look for in your future residence.

My horoscope for February 26, 2014 stated: *"To build a house, you start from the ground up by laying a foundation. It's a good idea to take the time to prepare for a new project, initiative or commitment by carefully examining all the pros and cons ahead of time."* Truer words were never spoken. Taking the time at the beginning, to prepare for each step in the process, will save you many headaches as you go forward to the completion of your project.

For clarification, this is not a technical manual. It is meant to assist you in some of the many considerations that you will go through in the various phases of building a house. Put some fun into the project. Have some laughs. You will make mistakes, but they can be fixed. You will meet some wonderful and some not so wonderful people while going through the process. Some will become friends for life.

The average person goes to school, obtains an education, works, raises a family, retires, travels and then moves on to the next life. You should question the stage of life you are at before considering building or buying a house as that stage may dictate the requirements to meet your needs. Today it is rare for a family to be raised in one house and remain there for the rest of their lives. As you go forward in life your wants and needs change and so do your requirements for a living space. What is important is to get the space you require, in order to carry out and make your everyday living comfortable and enjoyable.

Perhaps in the initial stages of your progression through life, before considering building, you may consider a stepping stone with the purchase of a condominium or townhouse for your housing needs.

Photo – Trailwood Place Townhouses

As time goes forward, your needs and desires may change and at that time consideration will be given to the next step in your residential accommodation needs.

One good piece of advice, before you even start is to retain a lawyer whose practice is focused in real estate will be able to work with you throughout the entire process from purchasing the property to finalizing any financial requirements.

In the end, this book will not answer all your questions. It is meant to provide some insight into the many aspects of the construction of a house that will, hopefully, meet most of your needs and wants. For most people, a house is the largest single investment they will make during their lifetime. This is not a decision to be taken lightly.

For more technical information on construction types or materials, do your research well to find what works best in your location. Do not be afraid to ask questions. As we all know; there is no such thing as a stupid question. So let's get started, and review some of the potential pitfalls, sequences, materials, options and issues that may arise during your project.

1. Site

Urban vs Rural

THE VERY FIRST step in building a house is to select the site or location where you wish to live. This may dictate how the house should be located and constructed. Selecting an urban setting versus a rural setting is an individual choice and there are advantages and disadvantages to both. An urban site will most likely have the essential services installed in the street, such as sewer, water, fire protection, and electrical services. A rural site may not have any of these services. In this case they will have to be constructed on-site. This would be a well – dug or drilled - a septic system – contour trench or septic field or other approved system, and perhaps the necessary electrical systems. The cost of the site may dictate the favorable option for your location. But keep in mind, the cost of the site, fully serviced, is what constitutes the total cost. So once you take the cost of the land, legal fees, septic system, water system, and the cost to get power to your location, and set that cost against an urban property that may include these features, then you will have the total cost for your chosen site, before life cycle costs.

The annual cost of taxes and water for a rural property will most likely be less than that of an urban property. But there is also the cost of travel - for the construction phase, day to day for work, or basic shopping and the distance required to be traveled – these will contribute to the actual cost of location. The simple point is that the cost of the property alone is only one of the many factors that go into the cost of building a house. It is most likely one the more significant costs that you will expense for your home project and one not to be taken lightly.

Further, your location in the world will also dictate the climate that you will have to deal with not only in the design, but in your heating or cooling requirements. If you Google world climate maps and know your specific location, you will get a very good idea of the particular climatic conditions that you will have to deal with on your chosen site.

Costs

The Site Sample Cost Comparison Table 1.1 below illustrates some possible cost parameters to consider when you locate your desired site.

1.1 Table - Site Sample Cost Comparison

Sample Items	Urban	Rural
Property Cost	$ 150,000	$ 75,000
Surveyor	$ 2,500	$ 2,500
Legal	$ 500	$ 500
Site Clearing	$ 500	$ 2,500
Taxes	$ 5,000	$ 2,500
Septic System	$ -	$ 12,000
Well and Purification	$ -	$ 4,000
Power	$ -	$ 5,000
Insurance	$ 2,000	$ 3,000
Annual Gas for Vehicle	$ 640	$ 6,400
Vehicle Maintenance	$ 2,000	$ 6,000
Parking	$ 2,000	$ 2,000
Total	$ 165,140	$ 121,400

It is not of any parcel of land in particular, but the table is used to illustrate that the cost of the site alone is not the only factor to consider when buying a building lot. Furthermore the cost of septic systems and a well will depend on the soil conditions of your chosen site.

A future consideration may be insurance for the property, be it rural or urban and will factor into your life cycle costs. A rural site with a fire hydrant beyond a prescribed distance from the site or a fire hall beyond a prescribed distance may result in an increase in the insurance for your home. Also, there is a trend today to include sewer backup insurance as part of your home package, and if you locate in a low area this may be an issue. Your insurance agent can advise on these items. At this point it may come down to the desire to have more land, or water frontage than an urban lot. This is a personal choice and one best left to you the individual, but one that should be considered when purchasing your preferred property.

Assumptions:	1. Urban drive to work 5 miles/8 kms
	2. Rural drive to work 50 miles/80 kms
	3. Cost of gas $1.25/Liter or $3.60/gallon
	4. Distance to shopping, urban 2.5 miles/4 kms
	5. Distance to shopping, rural 10 miles/16 kms
	6. Annual Vehicle maintenance, urban, $2,000
	7. Annual Vehicle maintenance, rural, $6,000
	8. Average miles/kms per gallon/liter 20/6.25

Then there are the life cycle costs. See Site Sample Cost Comparison Table 1.2 of hypothetical costs over a ten year period assuming that original costs do not increase. It is interesting to see that the additional costs of travel and insurance will increase substantially to the point that the lot at a lower cost originally becomes the more expensive option in the long term. So there are lots of things to consider when locating your future home site if cost and future costs are a factor in your overall decision.

If the cost of living is an important factor in order for you to maintain your lifestyle, then you must consider what costs you are prepared to pay to locate in an area where it will eventually cost you more to live. Sometimes the basic facts, when presented in a logical manner can help you make a decision that will affect you for the rest of your time living on that site. If this home is to be "a stepping stone" to another form of lodging, then, if in a rural setting, it will be important to determine the marketability.

1.2 Table - Site Sample Cost Comparison (Ten Years Period)

Sample Items	Urban	Rural
Taxes	$ 50,000	$ 25,000
Insurance	$ 20,000	$ 30,000
Gas for Vehicle	$ 6,400	$ 64,000
Vehicle Maintenance	$ 10,000	$ 60,000
Parking at the Office	$ 10,000	$ 10,000
Total	$ 96,400	$ 189,000

Other considerations when selecting a site include: vegetation - soil depth to bedrock - soil type - type of bedrock - ease of excavation – slope - and the presence a wet area - such as a (marsh - bog or - water course).

Vegetation

If the trees on the site you are considering are in a healthy condition, this may suggest that the soil below is good for growing, and perhaps easy for excavation. A test pit, (actually digging a hole on the property to determine how deep the soil is) - can be part of your purchase and sales agreement. Although it would be your cost, it can provide valuable information.

And then there is always the unknown. Once, when adding a small addition to an existing home and after having hand dug the excavation for the foundation, I encountered a problem. The excavation was over 4 ½ feet deep and in our climate that was 6 inches below typical frost limits. Thinking it was finished, I dropped a pry bar into the excavated area and it sank another eighteen inches.

The unknown in this case, was that the home was built in an area that once was a marsh, and what the pry bar went through was a layer of dried sphagnum moss. At least it hit good solid ground and we were able to complete the project without any further problems.

Soil Depth to Bedrock

Another important factor is the depth to bedrock on the site. If you are thinking of a full basement and bedrock is very close to the surface, then you should expect a significant increase in cost for excavation. Perhaps the site has bedrock at a level of 5'-0" below the surface. Should this be the case, and you are planning to build a split level home then this may not be an issue as your excavation would not be into the bedrock. In fact, it would form a solid base for the foundation of your home. This is a good example of where a test pit may be desirable before purchasing the property.

Soil Type

Clay type soils can be an issue for drainage and landscaping, since they do not allow percolation of water into the soil easily as do other soil types. A sandy loam soil type will usually allow drainage easily and be easy for the excavation phase. There are many variations of soil types and this factor is worthy of proper investigation. The type of soil may dictate the type or design for an on-site sewage treatment system. Sometimes the site will be a sandy gravel mix, making for excellent drainage and excavation. Most jurisdictions will have soil maps available for review of the specific soil types in the area of your possible site selection. The boundaries may differ from that on the maps provided, but they will be very close to the actual situation. Take these factors into consideration when purchasing your property. This information is valuable and can save money in the construction stage.

Type of Bedrock

There are many different types of bedrock and boulders in this world. The type, if any, on your chosen site, can increase the cost of construction, should blasting be required for removal. Some types can be removed with regular excavation or use of a breaker. A breaker can increase the cost of construction, but usually costs less than that of blasting.

For example, if the home you are planning to build requires a full basement, a test pit can determine if simple excavation will suffice or if blasting for rock removal is required. As mentioned blasting will increase the cost of construction and may include insurance costs for surrounding properties depending on site location. Should blasting be required, is the rock hard – like granite, or soft – like slate? Hard rock is more difficult to excavate. These site conditions will factor into the overall costs of your home. Be sure to investigate the potential for bedrock and which type during your purchase of your chosen site. Failure to do so can result in costs beyond your approved budget.

Ease of Excavation

This factor in choosing a site, for purposes of simplicity, may be broken down into three categories: excellent, average and difficult. A site that has excellent excavation capabilities would have no bedrock within the excavation limits and good soil for future landscaping. The average excavation of a site may encounter boulders and rocks that have to be trucked off site or used for landscaping. The difficult site would usually encounter bedrock within the designed excavation area, requiring blasting or a breaker for removal. When selecting your site keep these factors in mind. Of course this is only one of the many factors that require consideration when selecting a site.

Slope

What is the percentage of slope of your chosen site? 0 to 2% slope is relatively flat but it usually can result in drainage problems, such as getting the water away from your construction area. Do a little research of the history of the area and in particular the piece of property you are considering purchasing, it is worth the effort.

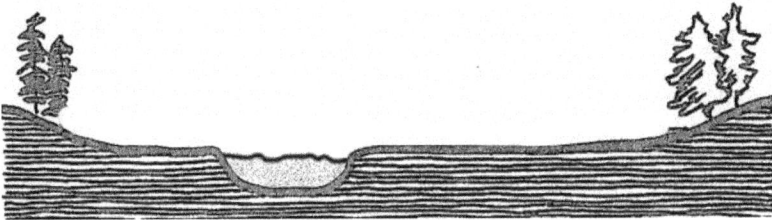

1.3 Sketch - 0 to 2% Slope

Heavy rains may cause water infiltration into your home. This is not desirable; it could be a floodplain area.

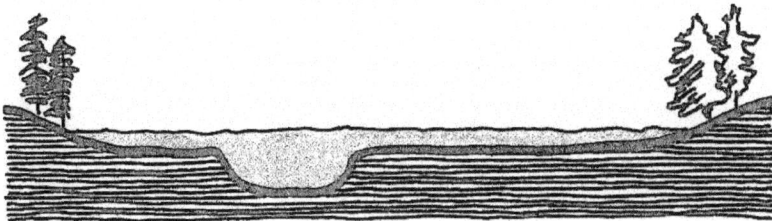

1.4 Sketch - 0 to 2% Floodplain

Investigate the area you are considering, and it particular, does it flood each year, especially in the spring during the annual run-off. These are the areas to be avoided for home construction.

A 3% to 5% slope will allow for ease of drainage around the building. However, you should also investigate what is constructed or may be constructed further up the slope to determine if it may have an effect on your home construction.

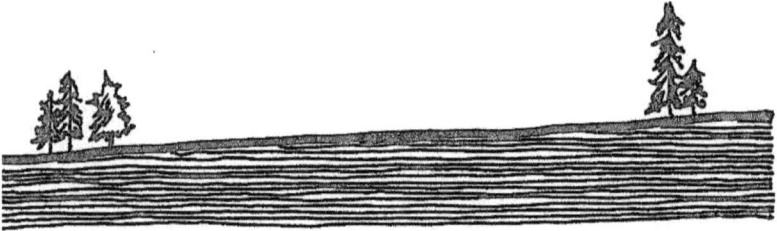

1.5 Sketch - 3 to 5% Slope

Slopes of 6% to 10%, may cause some construction issues, but are usually well within reason. While steeper slopes can provide interesting settings for a home they may also cause other problems. If you consider building on a slope, that decision warrants further consideration, as it may cause additional costs that you have not originally considered. But in defense of your decision, slopes can actually be a design feature of your home. It comes down to dollars available for construction and the desire to build on a sloped site.

An interesting site with some interesting natural features can add excitement to your project. The main point here is to do your research well in the beginning to avoid problems in the end. As you can see the slope of the land is an important part of the overall equation for locating a site for your home. The real key is drainage and drainage away from your home is the main issue. You can modify your chosen site with berms and swales to keep water away from your home.

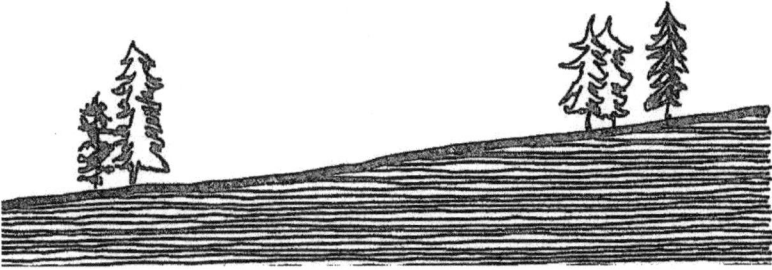

1.6 Sketch - 6 to 10% Slope

Berms are banks and swales are indentations to allow for water to run off the site in a controlled manner. If needed, they are usually fairly simple to construct and to maintain and can add to the landscape of your project. If you are uncertain as to the potential issues that may arise with your chosen site then ask a professional. They have the education and experience to evaluate these issues.

Earth-Sheltered Architecture

An old friend, who has since passed away, was Malcolm Wells. He was known as *"the father of modern earth-sheltered architecture"*. His theory was that man should not disturb the land by building on it, but should build under it. He had personally created some interesting buildings using this method of construction. And he used land that others would not consider building on. It is not for all but it is an option. And no, this would not be living like a rabbit in a hole in the ground. The designs I have seen have plenty of glass for view and natural light.

The roofs of this kind of building are generally protected from the sun's harsh rays with natural ground covers which provide wonderful colors during the various seasons.

For this type of construction, good drainage and slopes away from the built form are more than mandatory, they are essential. But think of it this way; it would obviously be a low maintenance type of

9

building. And to quote him from his website *"Build a strong waterproof building, insulate it, cover it with earth, and plant it with native plants"*.

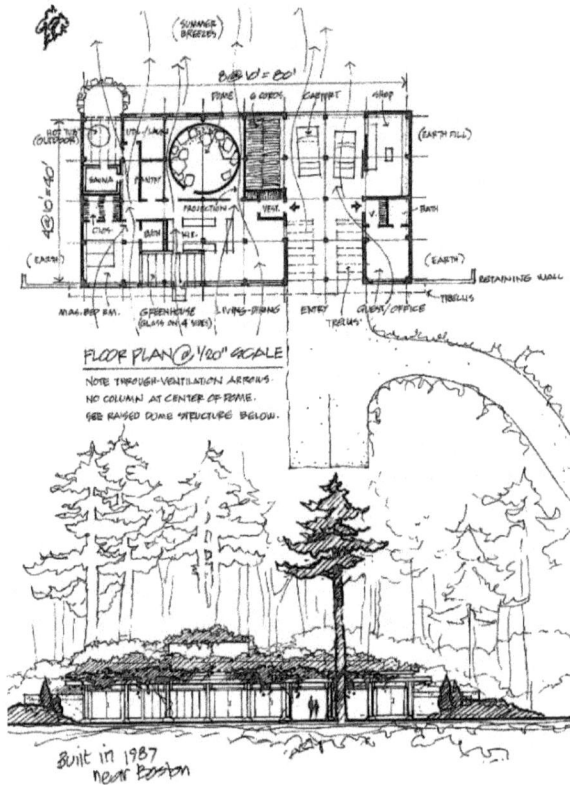

1.7 Drawing - Underground Home by Malcolm Wells

The ground offers great protection from the elements, both the summer's sun and the winter's cold, thereby reducing heating and cooling requirements, which are part of your operating costs. One of Malcolm's many concepts of earth sheltered buildings is illustrated on the previous page which is his sketch, used by permission.

This type of construction may be well suited for areas that experience tornadoes. Most wood frame structures cannot withstand these kinds of violent storms. Not only is there severe damage, but also injury or death.

Marshes, Bogs, Water Courses

Another item to consider is; as mentioned previously, does the property flood during spring runoff, or any other time of the year. There are many areas where homes or businesses have been built in areas that flood during certain times of the year. One can only imagine the headaches and problems of living in flood areas. We see them in the news each year.

Historically, as development progressed in any country, it was usually near a river or water body of some sort. Think of London, on the Thames, or Paris, on the Seine, or New York, on the Hudson, or Montreal on the St Lawrence, or Halifax on Halifax Harbor. At the time of these early settlements, water was the basic element required for travel; in a sense bodies of water were the original highways. However, over time the issue of flooding has become a problem in many countries. In 2013, Calgary, Alberta had a major flooding problem when the Bow River flooded. Some insurance companies would not honor the claims. In 2014 England experienced major flooding of several towns along the Thames and other rivers. There is also the issue of global warming to consider as the oceans rise over the forthcoming years. The issue of flooding is just another factor to keep in mind, when locating your ideal property. Flooding has also been increasing in some areas because greater amounts of paving do not leave enough porous areas to absorb rain water.

Wet areas, such as a stream, pond, lake or marsh may add an interesting feature to your property. Who would not like a stream or lake on or near their property? However, a marsh may cause a problem with mosquitos' during the summer months, and who likes mosquitos'?

11

Natural Land Capability

Each piece of property can be scored as to suitability for construction and it is something that should not be taken lightly. The issues mentioned above are some of the things that you want to avoid in pursuing your home construction project.

This is not rocket science. It is a simple exercise to go through to provide validity for the property you wish to build on. You can make up your own table of things to verify and set your own point value to each item.

Orientation

Another thing that you should consider is the orientation of the sun to your proposed site. Do you want the sun to rise in your front yard, or be in the back yard for most of the day? Think about how you like to spend your time on your property during your time of relaxation. BBQ's or family gatherings should be spent in an enjoyable environment and sunshine is an important factor. You may also be able to harness the sun with solar collectors that may benefit your operating costs. So do not overlook this potential when choosing your future home site.

The table used for this exercise utilizes the items that have been discussed previously in this chapter.

The points assigned do not have to be perfect as they have no real value other than to help determine the best possible sites from which to choose. Furthermore, it is a simple checklist to score items in a manner which may or may not increase construction costs.

A table such as this may assist you in the final selection of a site for your home. It includes most of the items that require consideration when selecting a site.

12

1.8 Table - Natural Land Capability

Item	Detail	Notes	Pts	Site 1	Site 2	Site 3
Services	Sewer		3	3		
	Water		3	3		
	Storm		3	3		
	Power		3	3	3	
	Tele C		3	3	3	
	Road		3	3	3	
Soil Depth to Bedrock	4'-0"		1		1	
	8'-0"		2	2		
	12'-0"		3			3
Soil Type	Type 1	Excellent	3			3
	Type 2	Average	2	2		
	Type 3	Poor	1		1	
Type of Bedrock	Granite		0			0
	Slate		2		2	
	None		4	4		
Ease of Excavation	Excellent		4	4		
	Average		2		2	
	Difficult		0			0
Slope	0 – 2%		0			
	3 – 5%		4	4		
	6 – 10%		3		3	
	11 – 15%		2			
	16% +		1			1
Marshes, Bogs, Water Courses	0%		3		3	
	35%		2	2		
	70%		1			1
TOTAL POINTS				36	21	8

Your particular site may require different point assignments. The site that has the most points would be the preferred site. This is a simple excise and may save you many dollars and frustration as you go through your house construction project.

In March of 2014, the mudslide near Oso in the state of Washington, USA was devastating. Many people lost their lives. This was a combination of soil conditions, slope and heavy rains.

If in doubt, be sure to research the area well and if the answers you are seeking are not forthcoming, perhaps you should look at an alternative site.

Vandalism

This is not something that you want to happen, but it can. While building some duplex units in a housing development, the contractor had just installed the windows and doors in one of the units. The next morning, when he returned to the site, all the windows and doors were gone. Construction insurance will help, but will not cover all the costs so investigate this aspect of your project in the beginning. Unless you can afford a watchman, while you are away from the site, it is best to be prepared for this possible intrusion on your project.

Our last home was in an urban area. Prior to starting construction, we sent a letter of introduction to our new neighbors, just to let them know what was happening and the tentative construction schedule. We found out afterwards that this gesture was greatly appreciated, plus the neighbors kept an eye on things when we were not on site.

2. Design and Contractor

Design

THERE ARE MANY ways to get your home designed. You can hire an architect, a home designer or pick a set of house plans from one of the many books that have house designs available. Or, you can design the house yourself based on your experiences. These are personal options and each one has its own merits. Think about how you want to use your home. Are you a budding chef? If so, then the kitchen may become a focal point in your home. Do you like to entertain? Perhaps your requirements here will require a larger space so guests can gather comfortably. Maybe you enjoy the privacy of a larger bathroom for soaking in the tub and reading a good book. Be sure to keep your wishes and desires in the foreground when designing or having your home designed. Your budget may dictate that not all you wish for is achievable, but at that point you would make the decisions based on valid information.

Designer

A registered architect has the professional training to undertake all aspects of your home design: the space program - concept drawings - construction documents - the bidding process - selecting the right contractor – inspections - and following it through to final completion. They will ensure that the home meets all the necessary building codes and regulations. An architect will guide you through each step of the process in a professional manner.

I am aware of one builder who says *"use of an architect will result in structures that are more interesting, unique, and more challenging and fun to build."*

A home designer has the ability to take your home requirements and put them into a set of drawings for you to take to a builder for construction.

There are some things you should check for when selecting designers: - how long have they been in business - can they supply references - what separates them from the competition - can they provide samples of their work - and who are the other professionals they work with - to name a few.

Space Program

The first thing anyone should start with is what is known as a 'Space Program'. This provides a list of the rooms or spaces that are desired for the home. This is where you avoid the problem of taking a standard set of house plans, which may be too small or too big for your requirements and start moving walls to get them where you think they should be. Such actions may also affect the structural components of that particular design.

So how many bedrooms, bathrooms and additional spaces do you need and require for your lifestyle. Remember, the extra rooms, bathrooms etc. that you have will need to be cleaned and maintained. However, you may be in a financial bracket where these points do not deserve consideration.

Think of the places you have lived prior to taking on your project. Write down what you liked and disliked about each of these places. Make this part of your space program. It will assist your designer in putting together your specific requirements. Perhaps you have had a fireplace in a family room and when in the kitchen or dining area you could not experience the fireplace due to the design. In addition make note of what you would like in your new home. While all the things you want may not be achievable, you should be able to find out the reasons why they cannot be included.

On the following page, 2.1 Table – Sample Space Program, you will note the list of proposed rooms for a sample home, the proposed size and area of the rooms and then the areas in the final design.

At the bottom of the Space Program table is the final area with the gross up to allow for corridors and space that is not labeled as a room in the table. This will get you thinking about how much space you will need for your lifestyle. Furthermore, if you have a good understanding as to typical costs per square foot in your area, then you can start to get an idea as to how much your home may cost to build. It is better to start with the space program long before you start to consider the layout of your home, because this, in a sense, is a shopping list of your particular needs and wants. Later this space program transforms into the design of your home in the form of drawings.

You may notice that the Family Room was deleted in the final space program. In this sample it was realized that the home was beyond the square footage allowable for the footprint on the chosen lot. Also, if your family is growing, you may wish to add another room or two now, or at least give consideration for this option. And if you have special needs, - handicap issues or a parent that may be living with you, - then this is the time to put it to your space program. After the home is built the cost rises sharply for these types of revisions.

Many people who do not work in the industry have difficulty determining if the spaces as shown on the plans they are viewing will meet their individual requirements. This is not a fault, but a fact. Let me digress for a minute and provide a story about my first clients who hired me to design their home. One of my neighbors wanted a home designed for him and his future family. Eager to do my first project I plunged in and worked with them through the design stages. The chosen drawing scale was ¼" equals 1'-0".

2.1 Table - SAMPLE SPACE PROGRAM (square feet)

ROOM	FEATURES	AREA (sq ft)	FINAL AREA
Living Room	Fireplace	192	276
	Entertainment		
	Open to Dining		
Dining Room	Open to Kitchen	168	168
	And Living		
Kitchen	Island cooktop	168	168
Entrance	Powder Room	100	91
	Closet		
Family	Pool Table	168	0
Master Bedroom	Dressing Room	144	160
	View to Backyard		
Dressing Room	Closets both sides	156	144
Master Bath	Shower, WC, Vanity	96	108
	Washer, Dryer closet		
Guest Bedroom	Bed, Dresser, Closet	120	120
Bedroom/Office	Office Area, Closet	120	120
Utility Room	HW Furnace, Air to Air	80	90
	HE, HW Tanks		
Outside Storage	Outside tools	100	90
Garage	Two cars, workshop	484	420
	Total Net Sq Ft	**2096**	**1955**
Gross up @35%	Corridors, closets, etc	733	684
Total Gross Sq Ft		**2829**	**2639**

A design grid of 4'-0"was utilized as most building materials use that module. Well, after a few schematic designs, a trend surfaced: they wanted the rooms larger. It became apparent to me that they were not aware of how the drawings actually translated into real space. Once the final design was agreed upon, and after checking the total area of the home as designed, my opinion was it would greatly exceed their budget. So, unknown to them at the time, the grid was changed from 4'-0" to a 3'-0", thereby reducing the size of the home by 25% and subsequently the cost by 25%. As the construction continued and as the home began to be closed in, the first comment they both made was *"that they did not realize the home was so big"*. I did not say anything at this stage. Five years passed before advising them that the size of the home was reduced by 25% by changing the grid size. At this point they thanked me, and based on that experience, I received a commission for another home at a later date.

Another friend, who did not require my experienced advice, built an A frame style home. The plans were selected from a home design book. The master bedroom was located on the second level, and when they moved in, the bed would not fit properly in the master bedroom because of the sloping walls in the A frame structure. All looked good on the plans, but consideration was not given to the combination of floor plan and roof slope when the building was completed.

Most people have difficulty with translating drawings into actual physical space. Think of it, a piece of paper, say 24" by 36", something you can roll up and put in the closet in your future study, lays out the design, room relationship and the sizes for your home.

In addition another danger is choosing a home design that does not fit on the site. They stand out like sore thumbs. Some examples: a full flight of stairs to the front door, a deck off the main living level two stories above the ground, a steep grade up or down to the garage, and similar issues. Many people find a house plan that they like and then chose a site that makes the construction process difficult. The point here is that the combination of the built structure to the chosen site is like a good marriage, they have to be compatible, in order to function as intended.

Home Design Books

Sometimes the chosen design from a home design book, may not meet local codes in the construction detail requirements, as these may vary in each jurisdiction. So before you purchase a home design from a book, ensure that the details provided: - such as joist spans, roof trusses, deck details, wall design, insulation requirements, - meet the codes in your area, or that modifications can be done to the plans to make them comply.

It is great to get ideas from books on design and from pictures as they do not lie, so they can be used to describe what you wish in your home. You can assemble a scrapbook, so to speak, of pictures of the exterior and interior to visually describe to your architect, home designer or contractor what it is that you would like to see in your home.

For this task there are numerous publications available. They can be found in local bookstores, on-line or in libraries. The more information that you can provide for your designer, the greater your chances of getting a house designed that will meet your needs and desires.

The issue here is how you communicate with your chosen home designer. The expression "garbage in garbage out" is valid in this instance. You stand a better chance to get what you want in your home if you have good communication with your architect or home designer.

The home below includes an extended roof shelter prior to the main point of entry intended to expresses its location upon your arrival. In this home the centerline of the view to the ocean, from the property, was halfway between east and south, or forty five degrees.

2.2 Photo – Entrance

This angle was used for the roof slope and many walls within the home were set at forty five degrees. The use of this angle created many areas of interest and allowed for unique positioning of artwork throughout the home.

Considerations for the Elderly

Should it become necessary to include an elderly person in your home then you have to give considerations to their needs. Will they be in a wheelchair or have other mobility issues? Will their bedroom be at ground level? Are they able to negotiate stairs? In addition should grab bars be installed in the bathroom? Is the bathroom close to their bedroom? Are the floors of a non-slip material? Also the less clutter in the living spaces that they will enjoy will improve their ability to move freely in the spaces.

22

Construction

Once you have finalized your home design, you are getting close to having it constructed. At this point you have to make some decisions: (a) are you going to physically build the home yourself? (b) are you going to only sub-contract certain aspects of the construction? or (c) are you going to find a contractor to build the house from beginning to completion, (known as the turn key approach). Your decision should be made based on your personal experiences in construction. Perhaps you have the skills to do the framing, boarding in, insulating, siding and roofing and then sub-contract the balance of the work. Whatever your decision; - use of contractor or sub-contractor - there are some questions that you should ask them before hiring.

Typically these questions are as follows;

- What is the main area of experience of the contractor or sub-contractor
- How many years has this contractor been in business
- Is he or she a member of a professional association
- Has he or she won any awards for their projects
- What is the warranty that they will provide for their work
- Will they provide a written contract for their work
- Will they provide references, that will enable you to verify their work experience
- Have they received certification in their line of work

You may also wish to check out the references provided and ask previous clients the following;

- Did he or she provided what was promised
- Were they well organized and did they provide professional service for the duration of the project
- What was the method of communication

- If they were to do the job again would they hire the same contractor

Should a potential contractor not be able to provide you with references of past projects, this may be a good indication that they could not satisfy past clients and perhaps they should be avoided.

Remember, this is your money that you will be spending and you want to be sure you spend it wisely.

3. Building Codes and Regulations

NO MATTER WHERE you build, you will have to work with local zoning, building codes and regulations. This is a good thing. They provide the standards that are required for basic good and approved construction practice. The building inspectors are very helpful and will provide good advice to you during the construction of your home. Depending on where you live, these codes and regulations will vary so it is best to get the most up to date documents for the ease of mind during construction. Your local building authority will have the most up to date requirements.

Zoning

The zoning requirements dictate what type of home can be constructed - single family, duplex, townhouse or apartment building. If you are thinking of making an application to change a zone to allow for single family home construction, be prepared for potential delays, as this process can take lots of time.

Regulations

The regulations set the requirements for construction on the site, such as setbacks from street: side yard distances - building height allowable – allowable side yard windows – allowable area of building - and maximum lot coverage, to name a few. It is recommended that you do a thorough review of the regulations required for your building location.

Building Codes

Building codes describe acceptable construction practices. This includes the minimum standards of construction allowable in your jurisdiction, such as: spans for structural members – thickness of sheathing materials – size of fasteners – standards for amount of insulation –mechanical and electrical requirements - requirements for fire separations – minimum room sizes – handicapped requirements, to name but a few. Again, it is recommended that you complete a thorough review of the building code for your area to ease issues during the construction phase. I am not going to say that this is interesting reading, in fact some is quite boring; however, it is mandatory that you follow the building code for your area, so it's best to be familiar with the requirements.

Building Permit

You most likely will have to make an application for a building permit and your drawings and specifications of your proposed home will be required. The purpose is to describe to the building officials what your intentions are for your proposed home. Typically the following is required: - foundation plan - floor plans - building section - wall section(s) – construction details – elevations – and site plan. In addition the cost of the building permit is usually based on the square footage or square meters that you intend to construct. This can vary from jurisdiction to jurisdiction as the standards may vary between each municipality. Be sure to get a copy of the specific requirements from your local municipality.

Inspections

There will be several inspection phases during the construction of your home. The first usually occurs after the footings are poured, and prior to completion of the foundation wall. Others typically happen during and after exterior wall construction, after the roof structure is placed, after the plumbing or electrical rough in, and then a

26

final inspection of all facets in the construction. The inspection stages may vary depending on your jurisdiction. You should find them both helpful and informative.

National Building Codes

Canada, the United States, Mexico, Europe and most countries have standardize Building Codes, which are revised as required, to set the standards for construction for that particular location. Most countries, provincial and state jurisdictions adopt these codes, some with minor revisions, as the minimum requirements for the building in that specific jurisdiction. These codes are revised every few years, but are not retroactive. So the codes and regulations in place, when you build your home or at receipt of a building permit will be the ones that you have to use for the construction of your home. While it is the law to build your home in accordance to the codes and regulations in place, it is also a good thing to fall back on should there be an issue when you wish to sell your home in the future.

4. Excavation

Clearing

THE FIRST THING required to start the construction is to clear the trees, from the proposed building area, if it has not already been done. This will usually require a few days. If you have some skill with a chainsaw, this is not a difficult task. Ensure you have the proper safety gear for the job. A few friends and your lot can be cleared in no time.

4.1 Photo– Friends Bob, author and Skip

However, save the beer for when the chainsaws have been put away for the day. Also you may be able to burn the debris from the cuttings on site if located in a rural setting. You may have to obtain a burn permit depending on the time of year and the jurisdiction. In an urban setting, you will most likely have to have the cut material trucked off site. This job may be undertaken with a chipper which would reduce the trees to chips for ease of transportation. Someone may want the wood from your site or you may wish to store it for a fireplace that you intend designing into your home. If storing for future use, ensure that it is outside the required area for construction as you do not want to move it more than once.

On-Site Toilet

If you are building in an urban area, with existing neighbors, it is highly advisable to rent a portable toilet for use by the workers that will be on site during construction. Or you could let them go to the local McDonald's, Robin's or Tim Horton's, but that will be time lost on the project and will most likely cost you more than the cost of providing the portable toilet. The convenience is worth the additional cost.

Foundation Layout

Once the lot or property is cleared it is ready to have the foundation laid out in accordance with the plans and to be sure that it is legally located on the property you purchased. In most jurisdictions, the layout must be within certain limits of the side-yards or neighboring property lines. For excavation purposes, the corners do not have to be exact because more excavation or less may be required depending on the lot and the slopes on the property involved.

Excavation

With the corners of the proposed home located, the excavation contractor can now begin his work. He would just need a rough layout for the foundation as it is necessary to cut back a bit more than the actual foundation size for ease of working by the foundation contractor.

The soil conditions will also be a factor in the size of the foundation area. As an example, if the site is rock, then there is not as much concern about the side banks of the excavated area collapsing. If the site has soils, such as the clay type, they may collapse during a rainstorm, and then the cut back may have to be greater to lessen this potential.

The excavated area has to be sized to accommodate the foundation formwork and keep the workers safe. This is more common sense then a rule, but one good rule. The sketches on the next page illustrate that the workers have a safe area in which to work on the building foundation.

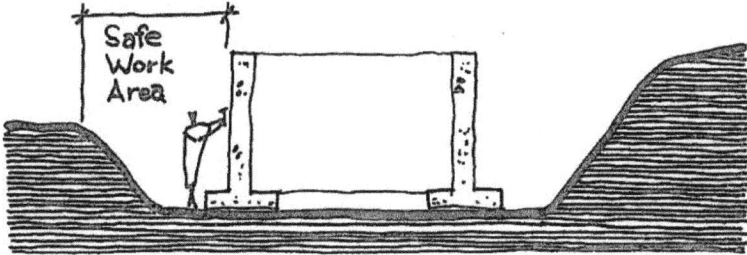

4.2 Sketch – Safe Working Area

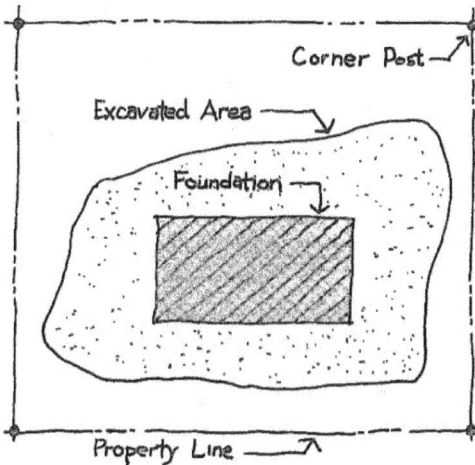

4.3 Sketch – Safe Working Excavation Area

Once the excavation is completed the foundation work can begin. The excavation contractor will also have to excavate for services lines, such as sewer, water, underground electrical wiring and communications, and anything else you may consider for this project. You may wish to run power and water for a future hot tub or a fountain or a post light. Now is the time to make these decisions as once all the equipment has left the site, just the cost to return increases costs.

The depth of the excavation for your foundation will depend on your type of soil and of course your design. Depth of foundation is dependent on the depth of frost in northern climates. However, some soil conditions or the design will require deeper excavation or construction with piles to provide a secure foundation. If you are building in an area of permafrost then you are into a whole new climate and professional advice should be sought.

During the excavation of one home I uncovered a nicely shaped granite boulder. I asked the excavation contractor to leave this boulder near the excavated area. After the foundation was completed and the floor slab in place, that boulder was carefully placed on the slab in the future living area. You guessed it; - it became quite the conversation piece. Now very few have something like that in their home.

Existing Trees

If you have trees on your site that you wish to retain, make sure to protect an area at least ten feet all around the tree trunk. It is best to stake this area and use surveyor's tape to identify that this area is not to be disturbed during excavation. This will save you money when undertaking your landscaping. Also, do not raise the soil around the trunk as this will most likely cause the tree to go into distress and perhaps fail. If you're landscaping raises above the base of the tree, then a well around the trunk will be required. Further, if you're landscaping will be below the level of the trunk be sure to maintain the original elevation with a raised planter around the tree. And even with this kind of attention, do not be surprised should your efforts be in vain. Trees, especially their root systems, do not like to be disturbed.

31

5. Foundation

Sub-Contractor

THE PEOPLE YOU hire may allow you to work with them to ease their workload and perhaps reduce your costs. Or they may let you work with them and increase their costs, depending on your skills. I was fortunate to have a trustworthy foundation contractor on my last house. Not only did he let me work with him, but he also reduced his costs due to my labor. And to show how trustworthy he was, he even reduced his bill further because his original estimate of concrete decreased. There are good guys out there; the trick is to find them.

On another occasion after I had purchased a lot with ocean frontage, and great orientation to the sun plus excellent water views, my preferred foundation contractor, mentioned above, was not available. He was taking his family on an extended vacation around the time that I required him on site. He suggested that someone else might be an alternative to himself. So wishing to proceed with this project, I contacted a few other foundation contractors. One came down to the site, looked at the property, looked at the other houses in the area and looked at the ocean view. He must have thought that this job would be his ticket to a winter vacation in Florida, because his price was almost three times what my preferred foundation contractor had quoted. The long and short of it was waiting until my contractor returned from his family vacation. So be careful and check your prices and the experience of the specific contractor.

Your foundation contractor should have the expertise to lay out the foundation according to your drawings; this would save the cost of a surveyor doing this work. It is important to have the property corner posts easily identifiable as this will make the work for you and the contractors easier.

The typical corner posts are usually pieces of iron rebar with a lead top and they are placed on the corners and intersections of the lot, usually at ground level so as not to become trip hazards. Sometimes they get buried by landscaping from previous construction projects near your site. Not to worry - they can be easily found by your surveyor. If the lot is large enough it may not be a concern as to where the home is located on the property, but remember to ensure that it is within the required side or street yard requirements of your local authorities.

Footings

The initial start of the foundation is what is known as the footings or spread footings.

5.1 Photo – Footings

This is a layer of concrete about twelve inches thick or more, and two to three times wider than your foundation wall, depending on soil-bearing conditions. They can be stepped should the excavated area require it.

The footings and walls may need reinforcement. This will depend on the height of the foundation wall, and the soils that are backfilled against it. Reinforcement is achieved with steel reinforcing bar. It comes in various sizes and your foundation design will have to take this into consideration.

Foundation Types

There are many materials for a house foundation. These are wood, concrete, concrete post, concrete block, stone, slab on grade, and insulated concrete forms (ICF), to name a few. One only has to look to homes of a century ago to see that stacked stone was a popular method for foundations. Having no personal experience with wood foundations, I cannot comment either way as to their cost or performance. Experience has been gained with the other types mentioned above and I have found each to perform very well in their particular application.

Concrete seems to be the product of choice for most foundations today.

Once your foundation is in place and you are ready to proceed to the next step in the process, it will be necessary for you to obtain a surveyor's location certificate, certifying the foundation is located on your property and within the front, rear and side yard requirements.

Let me digress again for a minute. Once I was called as an expert witness to a home under construction, at the foundation stage, where a problem was encountered. The foundation was for a split level home, so the foundation was only 4'-0" high on top of the footings. The contractor, in a rush to get the work done, stripped the foundation and backfilled earlier than the norm as the work was being carried out during the winter months.

The soil was of the clay type and so it held moisture. The backfilling was carried out in the late afternoon, and that night the temperature went below freezing. When the workers returned to the site an interesting situation had developed. The moisture in the clay type soil froze against the concrete wall. Now as you know, when water freezes, it expands.

Well, when the clay soil froze and adhered to the wall, it expanded and actually lifted the concrete foundation wall off the footings. You could pass a shovel handle under the wall between the footings. As the temperatures warmed up during the day, the wall settled back down and no harm was done. But never underestimate the power of frost, and clay soil. Further, do not be in a rush to complete various phases - problems can sometimes occur when things are rushed.

Formwork

There are several types of formwork. Each has its own advantages and the chosen method depends on you and what you want for your home.

5.2 Photo - Wall Formwork

Foundation formwork in the 1960's was tongue and groove boards, with wire ties to maintain the separation of them for the designed thickness of the wall, with removable spacers to maintain a consistency. These were removed as the level of concrete, rose within the wall formwork.

Before pouring the concrete, form oil is sprayed on the walls so that the concrete does not stick, to the wood. Once the wall is cured (this usually takes seven days), then the formwork can be stripped and is usually re-used later for framing or sub floors in the home.

For do-it-yourself people, with time on their hands, this may be the preferred method, but it is labor intensive. Today, most foundation formwork utilizes plywood panels with specific sized steel ties to maintain the designed wall thickness. These plywood panels can be re-used time and time again, making them cost effective for this type of work. (See Photo 5.2)

Insulated Concrete Forms (ICF) Foundations

The ICF method is becoming quite popular. Not only is it the foundation; it is also insulation at the same time. While typically a little more expensive than the standard house foundation, the long term insulating benefits are worth considering for the additional costs incurred at the outset.

They can also be used for the above-grade portion of your home. The one thing to remember about using ICF is that it is structural, and there may be difficulties when considering future additions or renovations. This factor is easy to overcome, if proper future design considerations are given prior to the walls being constructed. That is, to consider where future wall openings may be required. That will make the task easier should it become necessary in the future.

When backfilling against ICF walls, use a granular material and place a protection board against the insulation. Our friend, the sun, has a drastic effect on any type of rigid insulation and it must be protected or it will deteriorate very quickly.

Foundations

If you have exposed portions of the foundation in your design, you may think perhaps of adding some design features. This would be accomplished by adding some additional formwork before you pour the walls, to create some relief or unique design when completed. Remember, what you put on the formwork of the exterior wall will be in reverse when completed. So if you place a piece of wood on the exterior wall of the formwork, it will appear as an indentation when the wall is completed. So think about how you want that indentation to appear on the finished wall. This is illustrated in 5.3 Photo on the following page.

Another thing to think about is the placement of rigid insulation boards against your exterior foundation wall. This will slow down the heat transfer from the interior of your home and the foundation actually becomes a "heat sink" as it will retain some of the heat from the interior of your home.

5.3 Photo - Exposed Wall Detail

As mentioned previously, you will need to protect the exposed insulation, for the sun will break it down over time. You should also backfill with granular material to allow for good drainage away from your foundation. In addition, you may wish to consider placing a filter fabric between the gravel and the backfill material to keep soil from eventually filtering into the gravel.

Site Access

Today, concrete pumper trucks can make pouring concrete a simple task. Easy access to the site and location of where the concrete is being poured is a necessity. In years gone by, truck access had to be provided all around the foundation in order to get the concrete to where it was needed. If that was not possible then a wheelbarrow was used to move the concrete to where it was needed. Today's pumper trucks sure make this task easier.

All concrete trucks have to be able to clean their chute, after the pour, so the excess concrete does not set up in the truck. You will be a hero if you provide an area on your site where the excess concrete can be discharged and the chute can be washed.

6. Floors and Walls

ONCE YOU HAVE a solid base, - your foundation - you will be ready to construct the exterior walls and floors for your house in accordance with your chosen design. Depending on your location in the world, the exterior walls and roof will be your barrier between your interior environment and the exterior elements. If you are building in northern climates, your construction will differ from southern climates. So, to start with, you have to know your particular climate in order to properly choose your building materials, with insulation being one of the key factors. In northern climates insulation will help keep the cold out and retain the heat. In southern climates the reverse is true. The main objective here is to reduce air infiltration, to reduce energy use and to reduce required heating or cooling equipment size, thereby reducing the dollars needed to operate your home.

Insulation

Insulation provides the main source of heat loss reduction. The conventional method of evaluating the performance of insulation is to measure the R-value, the conductive heat flow resistance of the material. There are many different insulation materials on the market today - fiberglass batts, rigid boards, sprayed on and loose type to name a few. The heat flow through the insulation or R-value is usually placed on the packaging. Each material has a different R-value per inch of thickness. What is interesting is that more is not always better when it comes to the thickness of insulation used in your floor, wall or roof assemblies.

Obviously no insulation in anyone of these assemblies will result in 0% heat loss reduction. Typically adding 1" of insulation will reduce the heat flow to 20% of the total and at 5" of thickness, the heat flow is reduced further, down to 5% of the total. However, if you increase the insulation thickness above 5", say double it to 10", which is double the cost, it only provides a modest 2% decrease in heat flow reduction. Based on this observation, it is very difficult to justify the additional cost of adding insulation thickness much beyond 5", in most cases. However, you must check the actual material you are planning to use and to be sure that you will get the performance you require. This also depends on where you are located - in a cold climate, more insulation will be desired.

Vapor Barrier

The vapor barrier is installed to control the migration of water vapor. Think of this – it is below freezing on the outside, you are cooking or taking a shower on the inside. Where does that moisture go? Without a vapor barrier it would go into the wall assembly and freeze, then during a thaw it would cause moisture problems within the wall assembly. A vapor barrier keeps this air borne moisture inside the enclosed home until the air to air heat exchanger or open windows removes it. Careful attention has to be paid to the installation of the vapor barrier to ensure moisture within the wall does not become a problem.

Air Barrier

An air barrier is installed on the exterior side of the wall assembly. The intent is to control the amount of air entering the wall assembly. There are systems of materials designed and constructed to control airflow between conditioned spaces – heat or air conditioned interior space and an unconditioned space – exterior. Sometimes rigid insulation, depending on type, can act as the air barrier.

Wall and Roof

Another thing that you are trying to eliminate is air flow through any of the wall or roof assemblies. Reducing airflow will reduce heat loss or heat gain. In the 1960's typical exterior wall construction consisted of 2" x 4" studs, filled with R-12 batts insulation. One would expect about a 92% to 94% heat loss reduction through this wall assembly. However, consider this: if the wall studs are twisted, then there will be gaps where there is no insulation. Even though most wood studs today are kiln dried, they still will twist and thereby create an area of heat loss through your assembly. This fact is even true today when using 2" x 6" studs. While most suppliers strive to provide good products, there will always be some studs that are twisted and will create this problem, so pick your studs carefully.

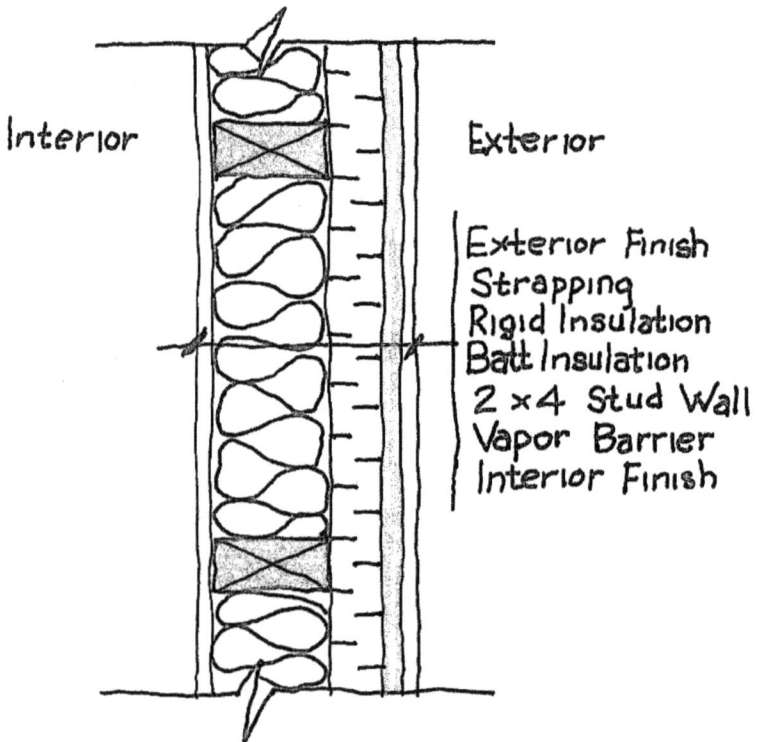

Interior

Exterior

Exterior Finish
Strapping
Rigid Insulation
Batt Insulation
2 x4 Stud Wall
Vapor Barrier
Interior Finish

6.1 Sketch – Method to Eliminate Thermal Bridging for Wall

Some lumber yards store their material outside and these may be subjected to ice and snow in the winter months. When they dry out, shrinkage and twisting can occur. This phenomenon also occurs with the insulation between roof trusses, as the trusses can twist. It is known as "thermal bridging" and one that can cost you money in additional energy use.

There are ways to remedy these problems. Use of the insulated concrete form (ICF) wall systems eliminates air flow through the wall assembly. But if you use 2" x 4" stud walls, with R-12 batts insulation and then place a layer of rigid insulation over the exterior of the studs, before applying your exterior finish, most all of this problem is eliminated. You can follow the same procedure below the roof trusses by placing a layer of rigid insulation to the bottom cord of the trusses. Use screws through the strapping and rigid insulation into the trusses. This will greatly reduce heat loss through the wall and ceiling assemblies. Remember, the strapping has to structurally support the ceiling finish, so proper connection of the strapping through the rigid insulation is a necessity.

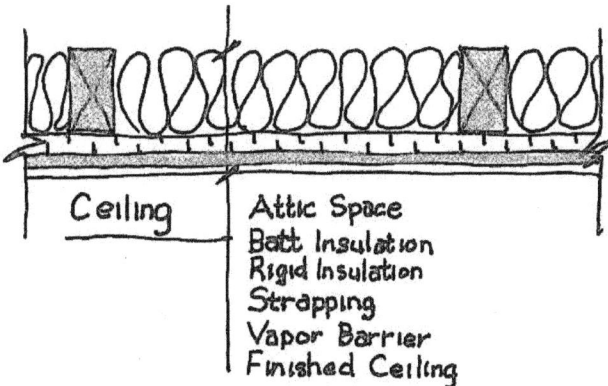

6.2 Sketch – Method to Eliminate Thermal Bridging for Ceiling

Metal Insulated Panels

In today's market, it is possible to purchase a factory insulated metal wall panel. This may be an option for your exterior walls. It is more of a commercial wall assembly, but can be used for residential construction and this may be something that you may wish to investigate further. These products will assist to decrease the issue of "thermal bridging", for your wall assemblies. These panels are available in various lengths and widths and are also available in many colors.

ICF Walls

The ICF walls are a system of formwork for reinforced concrete walls, mainly exterior and sometimes interior walls. The ICF forms are like Lego blocks. They inter-lock, are dry stacked, reinforcing bar is installed, during stacking and then they are filled with concrete.

Homes built with this system are built to last and I would suggest they retain their value longer. Furthermore they also mean significant savings in heating and cooling costs and less maintenance and repair costs over their lifetime.

6.3 Photo - Day of the Pour

They offer superior performance when it comes to thermal bridging, resulting in even temperatures throughout your home with reduced drafts and cold spots. Note in the following photo, bracing to

43

maintain door and window openings from bending, due to the pouring of the concrete.

These walls optimize energy performance. In addition they also dampen exterior noise, and add a fire protection benefit as most have a fire rating of about 4 hours. They also resist winds up to 250 mph. The cost can be slightly higher than standard wood framing, but the benefits can justify the expense. There are several manufacturers of these products and although the types vary, the end result is basically the same.

Concrete Block

Concrete block is a popular material for walls in the southern climates. It is in-expensive and easy to construct the required walls. Typically a stucco type finishes on the exterior and gypsum board on the interior. Depending on the climatic location, the application of the amount insulation will vary. These walls are strong and can support almost all roof loads with proper design.

Floors

Your framing of floors will vary depending on spans required, the weight or load that the floor will be subjected to, and the overall size of your home. Most homes will have a built-up beam, somewhere near the center and equal spans of joist across the built-up beam. This would be typical construction. Equal joist spans, or close to equal joist spans will dictate the depth of the joist required.

Your local codes will help in providing the required size of a built-up beam and allowable span of floor joist. Then the joists are spanned with boards or plywood to complete the sub floor system. Common practice today would be the use of T & G plywood where the T & G is known as tongue and grove. Thickness of the boards or T & G plywood is dependent on the spacing between the joists, typically sixteen or twentyfour inches on center.

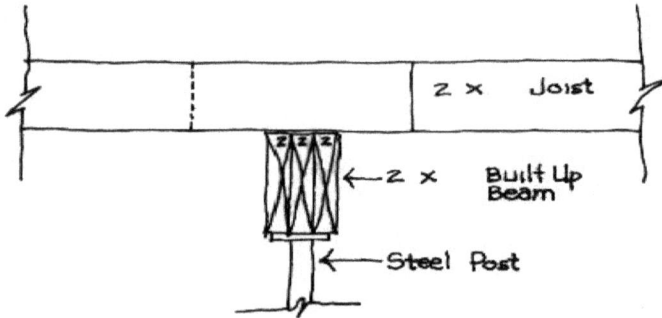

6.4 Sketch - Standard Framing

Floor finishes are applied on top of the sub floor.

Typical floor framing systems are illustrated in the sketches above and on the following pages. Each has its own merits and your chosen system will depend on availability of material, cost, and ease of erecting for your specific project.

There are floor assemblies that use what is known as wood I joist. These are a little more expensive, but can span greater distances with less material and may eliminate the need for a built up beam. This will of course depend on your chosen design and how the wood I span is designed for your floor system.

These are similar in shape to steel I beam only constructed of a top and bottom cord of solid wood and in most cases a web of oriented strand board (OSB), which is wood chips that are glued together under pressure making for a very strong product.

And there are also floor trusses, which can also span greater distances and allow for mechanical items to pass through them with ease.

Engineered lumber which is different than OSB board is another alternative. It is straighter, stronger and simple to use. It is made from wood chips and strands of wood, bonded together to make floor joists, beams, studs, trusses and other parts of your assembly.

45

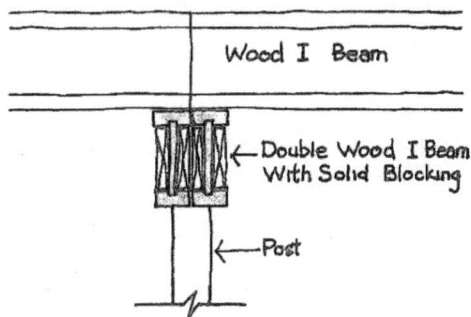

6.5 Sketch – Wood I Joist

They can usually span greater distances and support heavier loads. Depending on the availability of good material in your area, this may provide a better solution. I understand that there is some difficulty in driving nails in this material and perhaps drilling and bolting may be an acceptable alternative to nailing.

So there are lots of options for constructing a floor for your home. You may get the best deals from local suppliers so it is suggested that you investigate the possibilities available to you and then decide what floor system that you use.

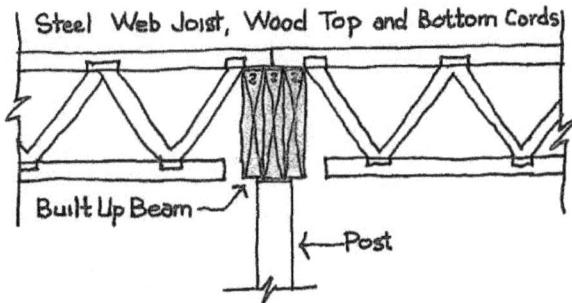

6.6 Sketch – Floor Truss

Decks

Decks are usually attached to the home for provision of access to the outside. Think of providing an opportunity to enjoy an outdoor environment with family and friends. Some decks are elevated, and some are at grade level. This will depend on how you wish to access the deck and your site conditions. Connection to the home's structure is a very important factor and one that cannot be taken lightly.

On the next few pages there are some possible methods for connecting the deck to your home. There are many possibilities for attachment. Keep in mind that the less area of attachment the less area there is for potential problems when replacement is required.

You might consider a limited attached area and then expand the deck area away from the building. You can get quite creative with deck design if you think about it. Consider to how you wish to use your deck - conversation areas, perhaps a fire pit, or for reading a good book. Also consider how to access the ground from the deck.

Let me digress again for a moment and share a story about a deck that was not constructed properly. An old friend on the South Shore of Nova Scotia, showed two of us around his property. He had built a boat shed with living quarters above. From the living quarters, there was access to a deck which had wonderful views of the cove in the area. When we walked out on the deck and as we were taking in the view of the water, the deck separated from the building, and we fell to the ground, about twelve feet below.

The owner broke his leg, I had some bad bruising and my other friend, was bruised but not too seriously. What had happened was caused by a classic design error. The owner had extended the built up beam, which supported the main living floor, through the building to the exterior.

47

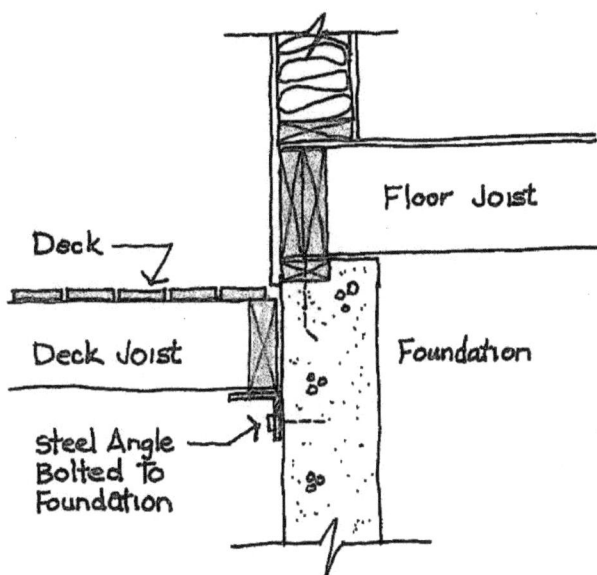

6.7 Sketch – Steel Angle Deck Support

Rainwater, running down the building exterior, over time rotted the built up beam at the face of the siding and when we walked out on the deck it gave way and the whole deck left the building. You might think that it would take a number of years for this to happen. In this case, it was only four years. We were all lucky that no one was seriously hurt. For some time afterwards, we were known as the **"Crash Deck Dummies"**.

So if you were thinking of using your interior built up beam to support your deck, forget it. It would be a very bad idea. How you connect your deck to your home is an important decision. You have to think that some time down the road it will have to be replaced and in doing so you do not want to have to replace siding or any structural part of your home. Perhaps you can do a detail that will allow structural support of your deck from the foundation wall (see 6.8 sketch).

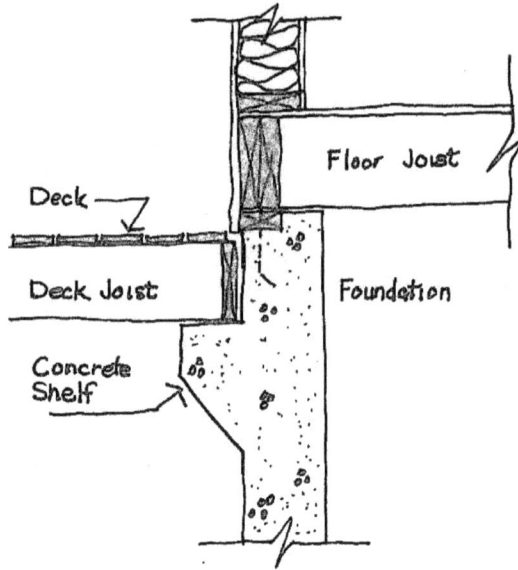

6.8 Sketch – Concrete Deck Support

Perhaps a check in the foundation wall is all that is needed for an independent deck attachment. Another method may be bolting a steel leger strip to the foundation (see 6.7 sketch) wall to allow for deck attachment.

It is strongly suggested that the deck connection to the home not go through any of the siding as this will be a potential area for rot and water damage. Also siding replacement may be required when it is time for the deck to be replaced. If you can avoid attachment to any of the structural wood components of your home, you may save yourself some headaches down the road.

Siding

When it comes to the exterior finish covering for your home, where do you start? There are so many combinations and permutations of materials that it is difficult to mention them all.

49

Basic materials used today are the following: wood, vinyl, aluminum siding, stone, brick, concrete, stucco, metal, glass and then the many combinations of those just mentioned. To me, the main concern is maintenance; who wants to put an exterior finish on a home that requires continual annual maintenance?

If you decide on brick, be sure to select from local suppliers. I am aware of one brick manufacturer from the interior of Canada who sold his product within the Maritimes. Unfortunately this brick could not stand up to the marine environment and it failed, resulting in several major lawsuits against the manufacturer.

If your home is to be located near a marine environment, it may require more maintenance then if it is located inland. Perhaps then it would be best to choose a material that can take whatever Mother Nature can dish out and still perform.

Again, check with local suppliers as they will be more knowledgeable about their product's performance.

Fascia and Soffits

The fascia and soffits of your home are located at the edge of your roof. The fascia is the vertical portion and the soffit is the overhang of your roof from the exterior wall. This overhang is important as it helps shed water from your roof away from the exterior wall. Width of the soffit will vary from region to region and usually depends on the amount of rainfall in your area. This is an area where maintenance can be an issue so chose your materials wisely. You can also install some light fixtures within your soffits which may enhance the visual appearance of your home or provide functional lighting as may be required.

Greenhouse

Think about having a greenhouse installed to your house. They can be custom constructed or pre-packaged from a greenhouse supplier.

They add additional living space for enjoyment earlier in the spring or later in the fall. Depending on your location, they may be too hot in the summer months, but good for getting plants started before being planted outside. In addition they can be designed as part of your home, or as an add-on at a later date.

6.9 Photo – Two Story Greenhouse

The photo above illustrates a two story greenhouse. This was designed as part of the overall house construction to provide a living space with southern exposure and view of the bay below. There is also access to a small viewing balcony from the second level master bedroom. This space was enjoyed by previous owners and now the current owners.

If you are considering this option, be sure to consider all the items you will need to supply: structural framing, lighting, duplex outlets, water, heating and cooling. Perhaps you will have doors to shut this space off from the rest of your home when weather or the season does not make it convenient for use. Frankly, this is suggested as there will be a significant heat build-up during the summer months. This will of course depend on the location. The further north you are, the actual use of this space may decrease.

One former client wanted a small greenhouse as part of the design of the home. This was the first insulated concrete form (ICF) home that I was involved with and we incorporated the greenhouse on the south side of the home. The wall between the greenhouse and the home was also of ICF construction. This wall helped reduce heat gain and loss into the main part of the house. This space provided the owner with natural warmth in the spring and fall and natural ventilation helped to cool the space when it got too warm in the summer months.

7. Roof

THE ROOF OF your home is your protection against the elements from the sky.

Materials

Again, there are many different materials for roofing - asphalt shingles, rubber membranes, PVC membranes, metal, clay tile, wood shingles, rubber shingles and thatched roofing - to name but a few. Another choice emerging today is the use of natural landscape materials on your roof. This will require additional structural support and it is recommended that you use the services of a professional for this type of roof design.

Asphalt Shingles

Most private dwellings use asphalt shingles on sloped roofs as the material of choice. Not only are they aesthetically pleasing, coming in many colors and styles; they are also fairly easy to install and repair. They are labor intensive, but if you are the builder, then the only concern should be proper installation.

Another item to check is the lifespan of the chosen material. Asphalt shingles have different lifespans; such as, 20 year, 25 year and 30 year, and these should be considered when choosing this material. The longer the lifespan usually means the thicker the shingle. Also check the manufacturer's specifications for connecting the shingles to the roof. Some will not warrant the installation if it is done with pneumatic nail guns. The reason here is that some of the pneumatic nail guns can put too much pressure behind the fastener and actually break the asphalt shingle. This may allow wind damage, as the shingles could actually blow off the roof in storms, and that is the last thing you want to happen.

Depending on the chosen home design, your roof may have many peaks (hips) and valleys. Aesthetically these will add character to your home and may just set it apart from the others in your neighborhood. However, these areas require special attention to ensure against leaking. Ice and water shield material placed in these areas, as per manufacturers specifications, will ease potential trouble.

Clay Tiles

Clay tiles are used for roofing mainly in southern climates. They last up to twenty five years. The cost to install is in the order of twice that of asphalt shingles. The tiles themselves actually leak in heavy rains, but the waterproof membrane installed below sheds the water. Over time the heat build-up causes the membrane to break down and that is when the leaks start and replacement is required. Aesthetically they are a very pleasing roofing material.

Metal

Metal roofing is becoming very popular because of the long life that it provides. Some manufacturers will give a fifty year warranty for their product. They also have a very large range of colors and styles to choose from.

Ventilation

Ventilation of your roof area is a very important part of the construction process. Typically the amount of ventilation is 1/300 of your roof area. I found this out the hard way. While building one house the concern was about the aesthetics of the soffits and I neglected this ventilation standard. More ventilation area was installed than required. While some may think this is a good thing - that more is better. In this case it certainly was not. While installing the insulation between the roof joists, on a day when there was blowing snow, it actually began to snow inside the attic.

To explain: on that particular day, the snow was blowing horizontally and when it hit the side of the home, the additional ventilation area actually sucked the snow inside. After some quick calculations, I reduced the roof ventilation and this problem was eliminated. Fortunately the error was caught in time and minimal damage occurred. A good lesson learned for future work!

The soffit is the usual location for venting your roof. If you plan on constructing your own soffits, then do you calculations carefully to ensure adequate roof ventilation. Make sure to cover any openings with a screen material to keep small animals from accessing your interior roof area, as they can be a nuisance. If you are purchasing pre-vented soffits such as metal or vinyl, they have pre-stamped ventilation installed. However, you still will have to do some calculations as the amount of ventilation varies in some of these products. And remember also, the product manufacturer of the soffit material does not know your particular home design.

Today there are also ridge vents that are installed on the ridge of your roof and then covered with shingles to match the aesthetic of your roof. These work very well, and may be a code requirement in your area.

Low Sloped Roofs

Flat or low sloped roofs can be waterproofed with an EPDM rubber sheet material, PVC, or a two ply modified asphalt system. All these products work very well when applied in accordance with manufacturer's specifications.

Unfortunately, our very good friend, the sun, does most of the damage to a roof, as over time, it breaks the material down. Manufacturers' stated life expectancies for the material are fairly accurate, and should be respected and monitored during your time in your home. When it comes to roofing, shortcuts are not recommended, simply because serious damage can occur when your roof leaks. And you may not even be aware of where the leak is occurring while considerable water damage is taking place.

Green Roof

If you do plan to use a "Green" roof, then do your research as to the required details. First, the roof structure will have to be designed to hold the additional weight. Your waterproof membrane, in this case, will be under earth and some type of ground cover, so any repairs will be a little more difficult, but your waterproof membrane will be covered, so the sun will not be able to do much damage from an ultra violet light point of view, and this may result in a longer lifespan for the roofing material. While I like the idea of a green roof, I would not consider putting grass in this location (very hard to mow when required). Think of local plants that will provide color and require minimal maintenance.

8. Windows and Doors

THE WINDOWS AND doors of your home are not only functional but they also provide an aesthetic. Their location should be important to any homeowner. The doors are to provide access to the home for both you and your friends: to allow in those you want, and to keep out those you don't want. The windows provide natural light, views and in some cases means of egress in the unlikely event of a fire.

Windows

When it comes to windows, they are pretty basic - frame and glass. The double pane glazing is one of the best and most cost effective ways to go. You can add argon gas and solar tinting to assist in the prevention of heat gain and both of these are good options to consider. The double pane glazing has an R-value in the range of 1.5. Triple glazing is in the range of a 1.75 R-value, but at an increase in cost.

There is a new product on the market called Solera Lighting by Advanced Glazings. The insulating value provides 3 to 6 times the normal insulating value. The glazing is a thicker panel than normal double or triple glazing units. They are usually installed in an aluminum frame system. It is not a vision panel, but it does provide an increase in illumination through the product, thereby decreasing the need for artificial lighting. This may be something to consider depending on your application.

Now as to frames, there are several options to consider. There are two basic types - fixed or operating. The operators are the difference. The typical type of operator is as follows: double-hung, casement, vertical slider, horizontal slider and tilt turn. These are usually a personal preference and will depend on the house design as to which option is chosen. The window frames can be made of wood, polyvinyl chloride (PVC), aluminum, or fiberglass. If you are a low maintenance type of person, the frame material chosen would be one that needs little or no maintenance. Wood window frames will require maintenance such as painting or staining to keep them in good shape; PVC, aluminum or fiberglass will require minimal maintenance. Again it will come down to cost of the desired product, and the aesthetic desired by you the homeowner.

Most jurisdictions now require a window in a bedroom to be sized as a means of egress in the event of an emergency. This is a good thing as should there be a fire, and you have to exit the home, you will want to do it in the most expedient manner possible.

Doors

Doors come in all sizes and materials. Typical door materials are wood, metal, or fiberglass with numerous window configurations. Door design is a personal matter. Size is another issue. If your home is a retirement home, then you may want to consider door width sized to allow a wheelchair or striker bed in the event that they become a necessity. Also if the door width is larger than the standard sizes, then moving household items, such as furniture, or appliances in and out is not as difficult. The cost of a door slightly wider than the typical door size is not excessive. However, stick to the standard door sizes available as custom doors can be expensive.

Most doors are 6'-8" in height, but they can be higher, should you desire. This will depend on the design that you are trying to achieve. Glazing in doors may also be desirable in certain locations, so that is something else to consider.

Doors are meant to close a room off from view, or for privacy, or for security reasons. A wider door does not cost that much more as long as you chose from standard door sizes. Doors can be solid wood, metal insulated or composite materials. Exterior doors are usually metal insulated and they come in a variety of finishes and designs. Your local building supply dealer can provide you with catalogues for viewing the many choices available. For your main entrance door you may wish to have a viewing panel. Another option would be glazed sidelights, allowing you to see who is on the exterior. The interior doors are usually hollow core, meaning that they are lighter and easier to handle. There are many styles and designs to choose from and there are catalogues available from your local building supply store. And of course, there are many different price ranges.

Skylights

Skylights offer a unique method for natural light to enter your home. Do your research here very well, for the last thing you need is a leaky skylight. The flashing of the skylight to the roof system is a major key to avoiding potential leaks. Avoid placing the skylight in an area where snow may build up, or ice damming may form as these provide a potential opportunity for leaking. Don't get me wrong, skylights are a great addition to any home. If you are not sure about proper installation, consider getting the right contractor to carry out this part of the work.

There is another product out there called "sun tubes", and they are another way to bring natural light into your home. You will not get a view of the heavens at night, but the natural daylight during the day is worth the effort.

Window and Door Schedule

Once your design is completed it is a good thing to do a window and door schedule. With this schedule you can do your shopping for windows, doors and skylights in accordance with your design. On the next page is a sample Window and Door Schedule. You will note that it gives the rough opening sizes. Be sure to allow some space, usually 3/8" to ½" all around your window and door frame sizes to account for the construction, hence known as rough openings. Each window and door will have to be shimmed and leveled within the rough opening before final connections are completed.

After this task is completed, the space between has to be insulated to avoid cold drafts. This can be easily accomplished with spray expandable foams. However, be careful with some of the spray foams - should they expand significantly they may place additional pressure on the window frame and cause problems with opening and closing of the unit. Read the manufacturer's instructions carefully and follow the recommendations.

Your drawing elevations should have the windows, skylights and doors numbered such as W1, W2, S1 and D1, D2 and so on. This will allow you to know where each window, skylight and each type of door will be installed on the elevations of the home.

8.1 Table – Window and Door Schedule

Number	Rough Opening	Type	Quantity
W1	2' - 6" x 1'- 10"	F	7
W2	2' - 4" x 1' - 10"	F	1
W3	2' - 6" x 6' - 2"	F & C	5
W4	4' - 0" x 6' - 2"	F & C	1
W5	7' - 6" x 6' - 2"	F & C	1
W6	9' - 0" x 8' - 6"	F & AW	1
W7	12' - 0" x 8' - 6"	F & AW	1
W8	4' - 11" x 1' - 0"	F	1
S1	24" x 48"	S	9
D1	2' - 10" x 6' - 8"	D	3
G1	16'- 0" x 7'- 4"	G	1

Legend: F - Fixed

F & C - Fixed and Casement

F & AW - Fixed and Awning

S - Skylight

D - Door

G – Garage Door

9. Interior Walls

YOUR INTERIOR WALLS are fairly basic: they act as room dividers for privacy when needed, and they provide an opportunity for hanging artwork and other items.

Walls

They can have openings for functional purposes: doors, a server between the kitchen and dining area, or perhaps an interior window can be installed.

9.1 Photo – Entertainment Island

They do not have to go all the way to the ceiling or to the floor, provided structural issues are handled. There are many different things that you can do with them to meet your specific design or needs.

In the last home, that I built, there was an area where the walls did not go to the ceiling. It was actually an island (see 9.1 Photo) which contained the entertainment center, fireplace and wood box. Visually, you could not see over it, at normal eye level. It was functional and acted as a divider between the main living area and the bathroom, the guest room and the master bedroom. Plus it created some interest within the home.

Blocking

Probably the most important thing that can be said about interior walls, and for that matter, exterior walls, is *"blocking, blocking, blocking"*. Make sure that there is adequate blocking for fastening of many items, such as towel racks, gang light switches, benches, mirrors, wall mounted televisions, or anything that needs some sort of structural support within the wall. Nothing can be more frustrating than to try and hang something on a wall only to find there is no structural support for that item. Yes you may find a stud for support, but I can almost be guarantee it will not be in the right location. Or the studs are 16 inches on center and your item requires attachment at 24 inches on center. This will take careful consideration during the construction of the interior and exterior walls.

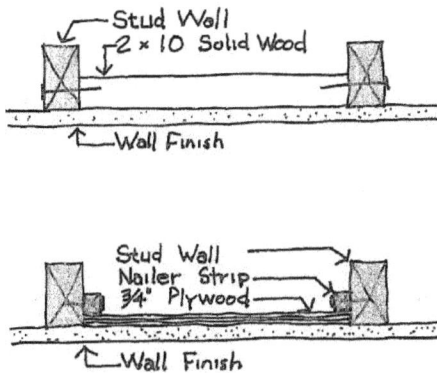

9.2 Sketch – Interior Blocking

When putting some blocking and additional structural support in the master bedroom wall of our last home for a future wall mounted television, my wife questioned this as she said we would not need a television in the bedroom. Now, she watches quite a few television shows in there. Blocking is not an expensive item, usually made from scraps of wood leftover from your construction. But you will be very thankful for it when you need it. So think about this important item during the interior framing of your home.

There are several ways to construct blocking and the illustrations on the previous page will provide some guidance.

Tools

Perhaps four basic tools that make the construction of the exterior and interior walls a little easier were a power nail gun, a cordless drill, a table saw and a cut-off saw. These tools are a very small investment for ease of construction during the building of your home. There are many other tools that you will need but these will depend on the specific job required.

Of course, if you can convince your significant other, a truck is also very valuable - one with a full box, so you can transport 4' – 0" x 8' – 0" sheets of material with relative ease.

10. Electrical

Temporary Power

ONE OF THE first things that you need to do - prior to almost anything else- is to provide temporary power to your site so that power is available for the various trades. This will involve your electrician early in the process as usually there are permits required and your local electrical authority will be involved in approving the location and set up prior to authorizing hook up.

There are two basic types of electrical hook ups, underground and overhead, neither of which requires further explanation. The earlier you have this installed the better for the overall project. This should be one of or I should say the first thing to be undertaken after the site is cleared of any of the trees and prior to bringing the excavator on site. It needs to be located in an area that will not impede the actual construction process but easy to access as needed.

Electrical Design

You would not expect to do your own electrical work unless, of course, you are an electrician. There are many qualified electricians available. Think about the many things you can do to enhance your home and the electrical systems. The key is to consider how you want to use the home. Think about where appliances may go, where you may want electrical outlets for lights, entertainment centers, lamps etc. There are codes which identify how many electrical outlets are required in each room, but they may not be located exactly where you will need them when the house is completed.

The codes are a very good guide, but are based on typical standards. Nothing is more annoying than wanting to plug an appliance in a wall outlet only to find out you will need an extension cord and it becomes visually unacceptable.

Power bars are a convenience but you may end up with electrical cords going everywhere. Adding additional electrical outlets may cost a little more during construction, but are worth every penny when they are needed. Be sure to give this item some thought when laying out where the outlets are on the walls of your home.

Lighting

The lighting of your home is very important. Good lighting allows you to carry out your day to day activities with ease. Think about where and how you wish to light your home. Typical homes have a single light fixture in the center of the ceiling of the room. This may not be where you will want your lighting for that room as it may not do the job for your uses. Think about how you wish to use that room and how you wish to have it lit. Each room will have different functions or be multi-functional. If your plans call for an office or work space, you will require good task lighting.

In addition kitchens require good lighting for food preparation which would be considered task lighting, whereas the dining area may require mood lighting. Workshops also require good task lighting for working with power tools and perhaps more outlets for your convenience. Think about where you want your light switches; is it a one way or two way circuit? That is do you wish to turn it on from one location and turn it off in another location. You may also want to have a light in a closet with the switch just outside, so you can see what you are looking for in a dark space. Imagine a light switch within the door frame of a closet, so the light automatically goes on when you open the door and off when you close it. A pot light is a good fixture for this location. And, no matter how much thought you put into this aspect of your home, don't be upset if you miss something. It is very hard to think of everything!

Switches and Outlets

When locating light switches and electrical outlets after the interior framing is completed, take a good black marker and go through your home, carefully marking on the studding where you want these devices. Not only will this get them where you want them, but it will greatly assist the electrician in his work. Plus you could install the required boxes in the locations you wish and the electrician can install the wiring, which may save some time and costs on his part. If you have an island in your design and it requires electrical outlets, be sure to consider this during construction, especially if your home is to be slab on grade. An attempt to enclose wiring after the fact will most likely not be easy. You will have to use what is known as conduit under the floor to the desired location. That is easy to do during construction, difficult to do after the fact.

Also think about your exterior use of electricity - say on the patio or deck, or perhaps a future fountain in your landscape plan. Maybe a hot tub or a heated pool may be something to consider. Now is the time to think about these things. Although they may be installed at a later date, the requirements for servicing them should be considered now.

Communications

In this day of wireless communications, it may not be necessary to install hard wire for telephone and internet. However, think about where your electrical room will be. You may also wish to think what else should go in this utility space; things like hot water tank, heating controls, air to air heat exchanger, communications equipment, etc. If it can be in a central location then you will have shorter runs for the wiring and greater ease for wireless communication. Also think about where your electrical entrance will be and if the wiring will be underground or overhead. If underground then the proper sized conduit will need to be installed early in the construction and taken to the utility room.

Imagine an entertainment center or centers in your home. Something you may wish to think about is additional speakers throughout your home. Places like your office, garage, patio, bathroom, etc. may be desirable. If you decide to do this additional feature, each space can have separate volume control. It is best to work with someone who is experienced in this line of work or a company that has experience in this area to ensure that you get the right products for the job.

Security Systems

A security system is an important feature in today's world. Do some research on the various companies that provide systems and investigate the options available? Do you want cameras? They can be useful and should you travel, with computers today you can do a visual check of your home while you are away. If you are away in the winter months and are concerned about the heating of your home, you can install an attachment to the security system that will send an alarm to the monitoring company that the temperature in the home has dropped below a certain level and someone will be contacted to investigate and correct the problem. This is known as a cold sensor. Another item is a water bug. It is placed on the floor in a low point of the home and if there is a leak or water infiltration then this will also send an alarm to your monitoring company. In some jurisdictions it is a requirement to have heat, smoke and CO detectors. There could be discounts on your insurance costs if you have these installed. Another item that may affect your insurance costs is a back water valve on your sewer system, to prevent sewer back-up. In all these cases it is best to review with your insurance agent.

Our last home had a security system installed within it. The home was constructed of ICF walls. Apparently, because some people did not like the sound of the siren, the security company installed the siren in the garage. The garage door did not have a door contact for the alarm as the control panel was between the garage and the inner house. So, after arriving home one day and had opened the garage door, then before entering the main house I decided to do some weeding. The storage shed door, which is part of the house, had a door contact, and without thinking, I got some tools out of the storage shed. That set off the alarm. However, I did not hear the siren because of the ICF walls. About ten minutes later, when returning to the garage, I found the security siren operating with the police and my insurance agent checking to see that there had not been a break-in. This incident provided me with the following information; proof that the ICF walls were sound proof and that the alarm worked. Just a word of caution: this is not recommended as a means to test your system.

Equipment Controls

From an energy saving point of view, it is important to have proper controls on the equipment in your home. Thermostats should be placed in areas that will best maintain the desired level of comfort for your home. Controls for your air-to-air heat exchanger should be installed in an accessible location to allow for ease of use. Again, should you travel; perhaps you may wish to monitor your home while away. There are computer programs available today that can perform this task. From a dashboard on your computer, you can monitor all the systems in your home to ensure that all is working well while you are away. Now there are also apps that can be installed on your smartphone and you can control your systems from anywhere on the planet.

Doorbell

One small item, but one not to be forgotten, is a doorbell. If you have a doorbell installed, locate the bell portion in a room where you will spend most of your time. Perhaps you will need two or three bells depending on the size of your home.

SO YOU WANT TO BUILD A HOUSE

Also, if the exterior bell button is equipped with a light then your visitors will have no problem finding it at night. There are some interesting doorbell covers for the exterior buttons that can add some interest to this item.

Interior Lighting

As mentioned previously, lighting is a very important feature of your home. Choosing the right fixture for the right application of your interior spaces is also very important. Think about how they are to be used - task lighting, mood lighting, ambient, functional or any combination of them. Lighting fixtures can be ceiling mounted, wall mounted, ceiling pot lights, and light valences, under kitchen cabinets or lamps. Today there are many different types of light fixtures to choose from, and they are available from many different sources.

The lamps for lighting are also important part of your design. Previously A-19 lamps were the typical standard light bulb or lamp. Today there are many different styles of lamps, shapes and sizes and all do a variety of tasks. The latest types of lighting lamps are Light Emitting Diodes or LED's. LED's use very little energy and will last for a very long time. We used LED's primarily in our last home. Changing a lamp should be a thing of the past for the balance of my lifetime. They do cost more than the average lighting lamp, but the simple fact of not having to replace them very often is a big saving. Also, think about the difficulty to change the lamps when they burn out. You don't want to be using ladders all the time to change a lighting fixture lamp. Locate the fixtures in an accessible location.

Exterior Lighting

Exterior lighting is also important, and can be accomplished in many ways. You can place pot lights in the soffits, wall sconces on the exterior walls, or an exterior light or lights on post or something similar. This will depend on your personal desires. Typically there should be a light over or near the front door and all exterior doors. Good for after daylight visitors and for you to see who is at the door. Think how you wish to switch these lights. Is the switch to be located by the front entrance door; is it to be on a timer or a solar switch? Those are personal choices, but the possibilities should be considered.

Think about your application of Christmas lights. Are you the type of person that puts up Christmas lights or lights for any special occasion? Then perhaps you may wish to consider placing a weatherproof duplex outlet in the soffit, with a switch inside, for two reasons. First, you will not have to go outside, to turn the lights on, particularly if it is a cold night, and second this eliminates the need for extension cords.

Also, if you do locate exterior lights in your soffits, give some thought as to how you plan on changing the lamps when needed. Perhaps if located near an operating window, you may be able to change the lamp without going outside.

Hopefully you will want to eliminate the phenomena known as "light pollution". This is outdoor lighting that interferes with the natural landscape and hides the night sky. Think about this when you choose your exterior lighting fixtures for your applications. Down lights are good examples of lighting that does not disturb the night sky.

11. Mechanical

THE BASIC MECHANICAL systems for your home include heating, cooling, ventilation, and plumbing.

Heating and Cooling

Your heating or cooling requirements will depend on the climatic zone where you build. There are many ways to heat your home: electric baseboard, electric hot water radiation, electric in-floor, oil furnace with baseboard radiation, natural gas furnace, propane gas furnace, heat pump, wood, and use of the sun via solar panels of some type. Your choice will depend on your specific requirements. If you are building in a northern climate and fuel is cost effective then an oil fired furnace may be the way to go. If you are building in a southern climate, and cooling is more of a requirement, then a heat pump may be the answer. Consider your particular location for choosing the best option in terms of operation and cost to operate.

A heat pump can provide both heating and cooling as required. It can be air- to-air, ground water sourced, or water sourced. It operates on electricity; does not burn anything, so no pollution and no chimney. It uses inside air, recirculates it, filters it and heats or cools it. You will have air conditioning in the summer and heating in the winter. It is a very efficient way to heat and cool and uses electricity as a means to operate. In some cases you may need additional means of heating, as back up, if in a cold climate.

Furthermore do some research here to get the system that will meet your needs? Do not think of just the cost to install; think of the long term cost to operate the chosen system. A few more dollars up front for a more cost effective system will save you dollars in the long run. Also consider the life span of the equipment, and the manufacturer.

Our last home utilized an electric boiler with an in-floor heating system. There were five zones within the home. The garage was also heated as time was spent in the workshop there. To make our system more cost effective we went with off-peak use of electricity. There was a timer placed on the controls that only allowed the heat to come on after 11:00pm and turned off at 7:00am. There was a battery back up on the timers in the event of power failure. Weekends and holidays were also off-peak periods, in our region. The supplier of electricity rewards those who used power during the off-peak periods with a lower rate. Your area may be different, but this is worth checking into before you make a decision. Peak periods are usually during the week when offices and other places of employment are demanding lots of power. The other reason the electrical heating was chosen was that you will almost never run out of electricity unless there is a power failure, which does not happen that often, plus it is a clean source of heat. Check with your local power provider to see if this may be an option for your location.

Ventilation

In most homes today an air to air heat exchanger is a requirement. Its prime purpose is to remove stale air and moisture from your home. Homes today, with energy efficiency in mind, use vapor barriers (discussed previously) to control the location of the dew point so that moisture in the air created from breathing, cooking and showers needs to be removed. They bring in fresh air to replace the air that is being removed and have several settings for different times of the year.

Plumbing

Your plumbing needs are pretty basic. You have to get water to certain locations such as kitchen, bathroom(s), laundry, and perhaps the garage. Consider where your utility room will be located as the shorter the runs of piping, the more efficient your systems may be. Long runs of hot water lines may take a little more time for the water to be hot enough for use if the line is run below the floor slab in a slab on grade home. Not a serious issue, just something to think about.

Drainage lines for water and sewer will require proper grades in order to drain properly. A professional plumber is your best bet in this regard, unless of course that is your trade, then you would have no problems. Your sewer lines will drain all waste from your home either to a municipal system or to a septic tank and field. If you are on an on-site system, your septic tank should be located in a place that is easy for a truck to access for the required cleaning (usually every five years), depending on the amount of use. From the septic tank there will be a drainage line to either a septic field or contour trench or whatever system is approved in your location.

Accidents can happen. We were in our last home for less than two weeks when we had a leak in the plumbing system. Fortunately, the shut-off valve was in an easy accessible location and our damage was minimal. The plumber had forgotten to crimp one of the water line connections, which was easily fixed as it was in an accessible location and his insurance covered the costs. Accidents can happen.

Oil Fuel

Heating with oil may be a good option, but check all the costs. In most areas now, you have to change the oil tank at least every ten years or perhaps longer if you use a fiberglass tank. This is to ease some of the environmental issues that are associated with an oil spill. You will also require a flue to remove the gases created from combustion.

In addition there may be an increase in insurance should you use a combustible fuel for heating. Perhaps your insurance agent can provide an opinion in regards to your location and the use of oil fired equipment.

We had an oil leak in one home we had purchased and it took several months for the odor to finally dissipate. A powder clothes washing detergent was used to soak up the oil and that helped eliminate the odor.

Solar

Solar heating is another source that is gaining popularity. Unfortunately, at this time the up-front costs are high. They will reduce however as time goes forward, so again, depending on the time you plan to build, your specific location and your region, this may be an option worth considering. Be sure to hire a person who has the proper credentials, to design your system, should you wish to go this route with your home.

Wood Heating

You may wish to consider a fireplace or woodstove in your home for heat and ambiance. Think about where you will want to store your dry firewood and make sure it is easily accessible as going outside and getting firewood that is wet or has snow on it is not really desirable. Wood storage inside the home near the fireplace is a good idea. Perhaps as you age the desire to lug firewood may not be something you wish to continue, so think of other options.

The fireplace we purchased can be converted to propane or natural gas at any time. Also give consideration to which room or rooms you may wish to have a fireplace installed. Think of how many times you may use it. To have one installed and not used is a waste of space and money. If near an outside wall, perhaps you could have a set of doors on the interior and exterior and store the wood in a small room between, thereby avoiding the necessity to go outside for your wood.

For insurance purposes your fireplace installation will need certification that it has been installed in accordance to manufacturer's specifications and to all building codes and regulations.

In addition, think about the necessary cleaning of your flue. The fewer the number of turns, the easier it will be to clean.

Fuel Appliances

Our last home had a propane cooktop in the kitchen. During construction we installed a sleeve under the floor slab, so the cooktop had an underground propane fuel line. I also extended this to the back patio for the Bar-B-Q and will never run out of fuel again as the appliances are serviced by a 350 pound propane tank which is filled by the propane provider. During construction, we also ran a sleeve for a propane line to the fireplace, for that time when we still want a fire but without the issues of wood.

12. Interior Finishes

THE INTERIOR FINISHES for your home encompass many choices - flooring, walls, ceilings, doors, furniture, light fixtures, color, mirrors, baseboards and trim, window treatments, accessories and layout - just to name the main ones. You will have to think about the ambience you are trying to create and what furnishings you will need to accomplish your wishes and desires.

Flooring

Flooring choices can be many - hardwood, softwood, laminate, carpet, carpet tile, ceramic tile, granite tile, linoleum, vinyl, and polished concrete -are some of the possibilities. Do you want a soft surface, such as carpet, or a hard surface such as hardwood or ceramic tile? In regards to carpet, there are too many choices, - to discuss further. In this instance, it is best to go to several carpet retailers and look what is available. The same is true for ceramic or type of hard tile. It is also true for hardwood or laminate flooring. Your choice will most likely depend on dollars available. Flooring is something that can be changed at a later date when finances are available. So you can save a few dollars here. Typically in kitchens, dining areas, bathrooms, and laundry areas, you would want a surface that is easy to clean, because you will most likely have spills in these areas. In your living room, family room and bedrooms, you may want a soft surface such as carpet.

In our last home, a retirement home, we installed polished concrete throughout. The diamond polisher put a very smooth finish on the floor. It is a popular floors finish in some large retail stores because it is very durable. You can add saw cuts to make it look like tile joints. We had a color added and the end result was a floor that we liked, but it may not be for all.

Should you choose this type of floor finish you will need to protect it during construction? One method of protection is to use sheets of plywood over the floor while the wallboard is being installed. After the wallboard installation is complete then the plywood can be used to sheath the interior garage walls which will allow for easier application of any fasteners.

Walls

Walls can be treated with several different finishes. The most typical and common practice is paint. There are many colors available, too numerous to discuss here. Again, you had best go to a paint store and make your choices. They will have paint samples available and you can take them home to view and study in the spaces for future application.

When it comes to paint, do not chose paint colors in the retail store as the color will appear different with the lighting conditions in your home. You should also consider how paint color flows from room to room, especially if you have an open floor plan. Add accent colors in carefully considered areas.

Another choice for wall covering is wallpaper. Again, there are many choices, and since interior finishes are a personal choice, it is best to go to a retail outlet to view the samples available. In some cases you may have a feature wall where you may wish to have a wood, stone or tile finish, and again there are many choices. So do your research here in terms of cost, and what type of finish you desire for the walls. Sometimes it is best to just go with a painted surface and later, when you have experienced your new surroundings, you may decide to change a wall finish, perhaps to suit a new piece of furniture.

So, when considering your colors, think of your furnishings as they are also part of your overall color scheme and should blend with your chosen colors. Furnishings include; furniture, flooring, rugs, and artwork. You should try to pull these things together in your choice of color or colors.

Ceilings

Typically ceilings are painted, but there are other possibilities. There are acoustical ceiling tiles, tin ceiling tiles, like those in the early 1900s, or plaster finishes. If you want something different, think outside the box. You may want to put a wood finish on the ceiling. Another option may be a sloped ceiling with some skylights to bring exterior light into your home. Check your local building codes to see if a particular fire rating for the chosen material is required. Your local building inspector can help you here.

Baseboards and Trim

The baseboards for your home can be different materials, such as wood, MDF (modified density fiberboard) vinyl, or hard tile.

I had a home once that was some fifty years old. Of course, wishing to leave my mark, there had to be some renovations. The baseboard and trim were made from wood with a unique design. As some baseboard and trim was needed to complete the renovation, I searched several building supply stores to try and find this particular baseboard and trim, without success. They just did not make it anymore. I went to a local manufacturer but the cost estimate to make what was needed was too high. Then I noticed that the interior of all the closets in the home had been trimmed out. I took some of that trim and baseboard from inside one of the closets to complete the project and when finished it appeared to be original construction. As a result of this experience, for our last home, the trim pattern was based on a simple design from birch hardwood and at any time, should more be required; it could be easily made for a perfect match.

Simple trim patterns are the easier to find when needed. Unless you are going with a natural wood product, a white trim will usually work the best. Most building supply depots have lots of selection for baseboard, door and window trim.

Hardware

The hardware in your home includes the door hinges, door handles, and cabinet hinges and handles. If you have an open floor plan, give consideration to matching the finish on these items to provide a consistency throughout the home. There are many styles and finishes and I would suggest that you go to a local building supplier and check as to what is available. Once you have selected your design for these items, it does not hurt to have a few extra ones in case one gets broken, or the chosen style is later discontinued by the manufacturer.

For your exterior doors, try to find a product that will withstand the weather and the elements of your location. Think about marine environments which can have a detrimental effect on the finishes. While polished brass may look good right out of the box, this finish does not take long to tarnish in marine environments.

Another product to consider is self-closing hinges. They are spring loaded and are great for the doors that should always be closed. Applications can be the entry door, back door or the door to the garage - any door you wish to self-close. You may have to go to a specialty hardware store to find these types of hinges, but you will find them very useful once installed. You may even consider using them on the interior doors of your home.

Windows

When considering your windows, think not only what it will look like from the interior, but also what it may look like from the exterior. In particular, think of the street side, - this gives the first impression of your home. There are many choices: - drapes and shears, Venetian blinds, shutters, many materials to choose from. They can be plain or colorful. For our last home we chose Venetian type blinds. They can be opened to let light in when wanted and closed when you do not want outsiders looking in.

Mirrors

Imagine mirrors which can increase light in a space and make it feel larger. Be careful where these are placed as you do not want to see the reflection of the dirty dishes in the kitchen or the mess in the laundry room. So, look at where you would place a mirror, put your back to the wall to see what the mirror will be reflecting, and then decide if that is the place for it.

Kitchen Cabinets

Your kitchen cabinets are important your kitchen design. If you are fortunate enough to have the talent, you can build them yourself, (provided you have the correct tools and skills to accomplish the task).

Today they are many options. There is usually a kitchen cabinet supply company near where you are building. They are worth a visit before you select your cabinets. Check out the many styles and materials available and also the hardware that can be provided. Some of the new hardware provides for self-closing drawers and cabinet doors. The hardware is quite sophisticated these days so be sure you give each type proper consideration before making your final choice.

Be sure that you have a set of drawings to give to cabinet manufacturers so that they can provide you with a firm quote for the supply and installation of your chosen cabinets. Your supplier can also work out the design with you and produce the necessary construction drawings, provided you give them the size where they have to work.

They can also manufacturer the bathroom vanities, should you need these in your design. Furthermore, if you need any kind of cabinet work for your closets, they can undertake these as well.

12.1 Photo – Kitchen Cabinets and Appliances

Appliances

Should you have an open floor plan, then your kitchen appliances will also be part of your interior finishes. So consider your overall color scheme when choosing your appliances.

A word of caution when choosing appliances - consider the warranty periods. Now I get to rant on a subject that has been an issue with me and appliance manufacturers.

In years past I have had appliances that have lasted some thirty five years. Today, that is not the case. Typical manufacturer warranties are for one year. Think of that. You spend thousands of dollars for something that is only warrantied for one year. You can get extended warranties, but you have to buy them. So you spend good money for an appliance and then have to spend more money for a warranty on something that should not have a functioning problem.

Unfortunately most appliance companies have gone "off shore" to have their products manufactured at a lower cost. Control in manufacture is not as good as it was and that is most likely why you have to purchase an extended warranty, so that if there is an issue, then you have coverage. This is unfortunate. When doing your research on appliances, be sure that you have a reputable manufacturer and one that will not hide behind a one year warranty.

In less than five years we have had three brand new appliances fail. One came with a five year warranty and was fixed, but we were without it for six weeks while it was away for repairs. Another had only forty two months of use and had two repairs in that time (which we paid for), and then we were told it would be cheaper to purchase a new one.

We have just finalized an ongoing battle with one manufacturer, over dual fridge and freezer units. It is not a simple matter of purchasing new units. They changed the size of the units and we may have been into kitchen cabinet changes with slightly over five years of use. I think you can understand our frustration with this matter. So do your research very well on these products and investigate warranties.

Artwork

Are you a collector of artwork? If you have some pieces of art that will need to be properly displayed, give this consideration in the design. Here is a case where you can construct an area, such as an indentation in a wall, or a raised platform, to display a piece of sculpture. As an example, in a corner, you can build a shelf area at forty five degrees to the walls for sculpture. You should also consider putting a light fixture above it, so you can highlight your chosen art.

Paintings on a wall may require special lighting. Think about this in your construction as the electrical cords for lights are not that attractive and will take away from your artwork. For example you could have a duplex outlet installed in the wall where you plan to hang a painting which will allow for a light fixture without the cords going down to the standard duplex outlet that is eighteen inches off the floor.

Remember the granite rock that I mentioned in Chapter 4 on excavation; the picture on the following page shows the rock and how it fits in the home as a piece of artwork. Examine also the wall indentation above it to accept artwork. Very easy to do when you consider these items before you construct, more difficult after construction is completed.

Artwork does not have to be just for the interior of your home. It can also be used on the exterior of your home either in gardens or around your deck or patio. Sculpture that is weather resistant is recommended, or perhaps you can move the works inside should you live in a harsh winter climate. There is no limit to what you can do; the only limitation is yourself. Perhaps you may show your wild side in the choice of artwork for your home and garden. Dare to be different! It is your life, so be the individual that you are.

12.2 Photo - Granite Boulder

Fireplace Finish

If you are planning on having a fireplace in your home, think about how you wish to show it. Brick, granite, tile etc. are all acceptable finishes. Should you have a fireplace in your home it may be a focal point in that particular room or part of combined spaces.

A number of years ago, my architectural firm had a commission to renovate a particular retail storefront. The existing exterior finish was Quebec Black granite, and it was to be replaced with a more modern storefront. After the contract was let, we questioned the contractor on his intentions with the granite after removal, and his response was that it was of no value to him. We asked if he would mind if we became responsible for removal from the site. He responded that he would advise of the day to be on site to take it away. We rented a truck, and arrived on site to load the granite as it was being removed. This also included the granite window sills and all the granite panels. We took them to a granite stone workshop where they were cut and polished to the design for a fireplace in one of the homes I built. The window sills became part of the hearth for the fireplace. Some pieces of granite were also used to enhance the arches to the next room. A picture of the finished fireplace is illustrated below. The end result: somebody's waste became a beautiful finish for a two sided fireplace.

12.3 Photo – Re-Used Granite for Fireplace Finish

Our current fireplace will take a log up to forty two inches long. We do enjoy a fire for the heat and the ambience. The finish around the fireplace is granite. When we found our preferred supplier we asked if there was stock left over from previous jobs that would be available at a lower price. Not only were we able to finish the fireplace; we also were able to do the vanities in the bathrooms with some left over product. There are great opportunities for finding suitable products for various uses in material that may otherwise just be thrown away.

Furnishings

The furniture that you place in your new home will also enhance your living space. Maybe it is time to get rid of that old wingback chair that your grandmother gave you and upgrade to something that fits into your new living space. Now don't go out and buy all new furniture just because this book says so. Think about what you want and need to make your living space comfortable for you, and within your price range. In our last home we had a dining room set that was in excellent condition and over thirty five years old, but unfortunately did not fit into our new décor. We waited for a few years before we decided it was time to change it and to get something that really complimented the overall design and layout of our home.

13. Landscaping

OK, YOUR HOUSE is finished, and you may or may not have moved in, but you have not finished yet. You need to decide what you to do for landscaping around your house. If you have an urban lot you may be restricted as to what you can do for landscaping. The restricted covenants or deed restrictions may require you to landscape in a manner that is similar to the other homes in the area so there is uniformity to the overall development. If you are located in a rural area, you most likely will not have any landscaping restrictions.

Driveway

Your driveway is the vehicle access to your property. Most houses have driveways that are straight off the street and in order to get back on the street you have to put your vehicle in reverse and back out onto the roadway. This may not be practical in some areas. Think about being able to turn around on your property that you can access the street, going forward. This may require more paving but leaving your property will be done in a safe manner. In addition your garage, should you have one, may not face the street, as per the following photo 13.1.

Yard

For our last home in an urban area, I, as a personal choice, did not want a lawn. In order to have a proper lawn, you have to fertilize, lime and water it to make the grass grow and when it grows then you have to cut it. That becomes a make-work project and one that is not to my liking. There is a cost and time commitment to properly fertilize, develop and then cut a lawn. As mentioned there is also a requirement to water your lawn during periods without rain, which can increase your costs for water and may be wasteful. My preference is to be on the golf course or fishing, so I choose not to put in a lawn.

Our driveway, walkways and patio areas, are concrete with aggregate stone finish. The stone provides a nice reddish color for the driveway. We also got, but didn't request, some raccoon foot prints in the driveway as one tried to cross while it was still wet cement. It makes for an interesting conversation piece.

13.1 Photo – Driveway, Landscaping and Birch Trees

On one side of our home we installed beach stone and the balance of the area is bark mulch, low ground covers and shrubs. At this point the shrubs are really starting to take shape and the ground covers have some colorful blooms in the spring and summer and maintenance is minimal - maintenance being weed removal, and refreshing the bark mulch every few years. Another advantage to the no lawn approach is that you will use no or fewer fertilizers, less water and you will have built a "green" environment.

Also you can see how the birch trees have been left at their original grade with use of a simple hand laid stone wall. As this house is elevated on the site, drainage is not an issue.

You may wish to have a lawn. There are three ways to achieve this – seed, hydro-seed or sod. If you plan on seeding, you will need, depending on your area, a certain amount of good topsoil to allow for the seed to take proper root. Depending on your location, this usually takes two full growing seasons, spring and fall. Another method for seeding is hydro-seeding. This is a method where fertilizers and grass seed are combined in a slurry which is then sprayed on your property. It is quicker than seeding and gives a green look almost immediately. The quickest way to a green lawn is to sod the area in question. It will be green quicker, but still requires the two full growing seasons for the sod to take proper root.

Trees

Consider the location of your lot that you may have trees or you may wish to plant trees. Visit your local garden center to see what is available and will grow in your area. Knowledge of your soil type will be a great asset. There are many variations of trees, shrubs and groundcovers available. Think about what you wish your property to look like a few years down the road. Most shrubs and ground covers take a few years to fill in. Go by suppliers instructions as to spacing and location.

For trees, that you wish to retain, it is very important not to disturb the existing root structure. In fact, it is best to leave the area un-disturbed at least ten feet all around the trunk. (See photo 13.1) If you find that your landscaping requires the area around the existing tree to be built up then create a well around the trunk so that it remains at the former grade level. This is important for the tree or trees to survive the construction around it. If you can, stake an area around the trees you wish to keep and put some kind of ribbon tape from stake to stake to identify the area you are trying to maintain at the existing grade.

Drainage

Think about how you wish to allow run-off from rainwater and melting snow, to drain away from your property. In some cases there may be a natural way to allow for drainage, such as a ditch to lead the runoff water to storm drains or to a natural watercourse. You do not want your construction to impede the flow of runoff water or to affect your neighbor's property. If you have an urban lot, you may be required to have eaves troughs around your roof to control roof rainwater. In this case the drains would lead to piped storm sewers. Should you have a larger rural property, this may not be as much of an issue. In some cases it may be as simple as depressing an area, known in the trade as a swale, between neighboring properties to allow for drainage to the urban installed systems. This is an important factor and must not be overlooked.

In our last home we had an interesting problem at one corner of the property. It was a natural low area and rainwater collected in that area. My neighbor's backyard would actually flood in heavy rains. Fortunately for me, this was a known fact before construction started. While the excavation contractor was on site, we approached our neighbor and discussed the possibility of installing a drywell on my property to hopefully ease the flooding issue. The excavation contractor dug a hole, in the low area, about twelve feet deep and then with a breaker, put some cracks in the rock. Next the hole was filled with 2 inch stone and this was also an area that was covered with stone in the final landscaping. So now the water had a place to go, flooding was all but eliminated and what did occur, in a very short time drained away.

Water will always seek the low area of your property, so ensure that it has a place to runoff without hampering any of your neighbor's properties.

Patio

Enjoying your patio or outside living space in the warm weather is a wonderful experience. This would be a great spot to locate your Bar-B-Que and to enjoy casual summer time outdoor dining. If you locate in an area where mosquitoes and other insects frequent your yard there are several items you can purchase to deal with these pesky insects. Some of these products are available from stores that sell camping equipment.

Patios have come a long way from the old 2'-0" by 2'-0" concrete pavers. You can pour in place a concrete patio during the construction process or you can use some of the many patio stones that are now available. It is suggested that you chose a color that is in the grey or tan tones as they will help create a neutral background for colorful furniture or perhaps some sculpture or other artworks. Think of low maintenance for this space. Patios are one of the higher expenses for outdoor living, but worth the additional costs and may actually be a selling feature when and if that becomes an option.

Furthermore they are great locations for outdoor fireplaces, a gathering space for many occasions. Some locations may restrict the use of wood fire pits and in this case one of the new propane fire pits may be an option. If you are thinking this way from the beginning, it might be feasible to run a propane or natural gas line to the appliance from your supply, especially if you are considering gas appliances for you home. You may also think of placing outside speakers from your sound system so you can enjoy music while outside.

Imagine a roof over your lawn furniture so you can sit outside on a warm day even if it is raining. Think of this roof as your umbrella for protection from the sun's rays. In addition, speakers can be installed for your listening pleasure. This may also be a good place to put the Bar-B-Que for weather protection.

Lighting

We talked about lighting in Chapter 11 on electrical; however, you may wish to think about some landscape lighting installed on your property. This will provide a nice ambience when you are using your property after the sun goes down for the evening. Think of walkway bollards, down lights and up lights. A solar switch may be appropriate to turn the lights on at dusk and off at first light in the morning. You may also wish to install a light pole or poles on your property to light your driveway and walkways. Imagine how you wish your property to look in the evening hours. Be sure to allow for adequate circuit breakers in your electrical panel and provide waterproof conduit for the wiring to the locations that you wish to illuminate.

14. Finances

UNLESS MONEY IS no object you will most likely be financing your house project.

Financing

You can shop around for the best deal, but usually the banking institution that you are currently dealing with will be the best place to start as they know your personal financial status. It is highly recommend that you do not start construction until you have secured the necessary financing to complete your project. Self-builds are considered one of the riskiest loans for a lending institution. Most banks do not wish to finance self-builds, so you will have to be properly prepared. Each country may have different versions of financing, but generally what is described on the following pages can be used as a guide.

Should you chose to hire a qualified contractor for your project he or she can assume financial responsibility for the project. In this case you would be expected to make payments at certain stages of the work or a final payment at the end of the project when 100% completed.

Qualifications

It is wise to be "pre-qualified" for the amount of loan you can service prior to finalizing your design. In fact this is probably one of the first steps that you should take and any financial institution will be happy to assist you with this step. This will avoid the issue of having a home designed beyond your financial means. Your financial institution will want to know your ability to repay and that you have good credit. They will want to know the combined income that is available to service the loan required to build the house. Once you have an amount of loan approved, that you can properly service, and you know the cost per square foot of construction for your chosen area, then you can work backwards to see if the loan will enable you to build the approximate size of house that you desire.

With this information you can start the design process for your home. When you have the design completed, then you can make application to your financial institution for the necessary funding. For this the financial institution will need the following: *a full set of plans, specifications and cost estimate*. With these documents they will be able to determine the value upon completion and the amount of loan to be serviced.

Also, the location of the proposed development will be part of the requirements as it will be part of the total value of the project. An assessment of the total project will be undertaken by the financial institution to see that your project meets their requirements and that financing will be acceptable.

Appliances such as washer, dryer, stove, refrigerator and dishwasher are not considered part of the mortgage assets for your home.

Types of Loans

The difference between a construction loan and a purchase loan is that there is an "interest only" phase on the construction loan. Typically this phase lasts approximately nine months, but may vary with prior approval. During this phase the borrower only pays interest on the amount of funds withdrawn. There will be little interest at first, but this will go up as more funds are withdrawn to pay for the completed construction.

In some locations or countries there are two different types of construction loans; single closing or double closing. Under a single closing loan you would only sign one set of documents for the "interest only" phase and then it automatically goes into monthly payments once it comes out of the interest only phase. The advantages are that you, the borrower, only have to sign one set of documents, and you lock the interest rate in at the beginning and it stays there until the loan matures. The other type is known as "double closing" which means you actually take out two loans. One loan is for the interest period only and the other loan is for amortization upon completion. The disadvantages here are there are two sets of documents to sign. In this case the rate for the final loan is then established at the time that loan is made. Perhaps you would only consider this if you believe that the interest rate may decrease around your scheduled completion time.

These discussions are best held with your chosen financial institution. They will be the governing factor when it comes to financing your project.

The other issue that makes construction lending risky is the possibility of a "mechanics lien" against the project. This would occur when a contractor does not get paid, as per his contract and a mechanics lien is placed on the property. They are meant to provide the contractor protection from not getting paid. Before each advance of funds a solicitor will confirm that there are no liens against the project. There may be a percentage holdback to ensure that various trades do not place a lien after the fact for non-payment. Should a lien exist, no further funds will be advanced until the lien is resolved. There may be delays and additional legal fees.

Once your loan is approved, then you can start the construction process. At various pre-determined stages in the construction process, the financial institution will undertake inspections to determine the stage of construction and the percentage of completion and then they will provide authorization for a draw against the approved loan. Typical stages are foundation, framing, roof tight, mechanical and electrical rough-ins, interior finishes, and 100% complete. These can vary from region to region, so be sure to request the actual stages of draws on your project from your financial institution.

Once the home is completed and ready for occupancy your mortgage details will be finalized. Perhaps you will also need an occupancy permit from your local municipality prior to moving in.

Drawings

The drawings for the home lay out the number and relationship of the rooms to be included in the construction. They will also describe what the house will look like when completed. They are an important link in the process and will act as the guide for the construction of the home. Plus they are necessary for your financial institution to set a value to the overall project. This was discussed in Chapter 2

Specifications

The specifications describe exactly what each part of the home will be when completed and how it is required to be put together. As an example, they will describe the type of foundation, type of framing, amount of insulation, heating system, light fixtures etc., etc. And as specifications, they will be more specific. Instead of "insulation in the wall", the specification would say something like "R-20 Fibreglass Batt Insulation". As you can see, this is more specific.

Cost Estimate

On the next page is a cost estimating format for you to examine. It may not cover all the items that you are considering for your home and should only act as a guide for your particular project. Note: it shows budget and then actual costs, to give you an idea of where things could go in terms of dollars spent. Some items were below budget and some were over the budgeted costs. This is typical in almost any project. Your budget must be prepared before you start the loan application process.

When you are actually constructing your home, you may change your mind on some items that will increase or decrease your final costs. This is typical of any construction project. In construction terms, these are known as "change orders", - a change from the original cost of the project. The change order would reflect the change in cost from the original contract, either an increase or decrease depending on the particular item or items changed.

An example could be a change from ceramic tile flooring to vinyl tile, which would typically be less than the original contract. These change orders may also have an effect on the final loan for your project. For example if you decrease the value of the approved construction drawings, specifications and cost estimate then you should expect a change in the final amount of loan.

The point is that the financial institution will only provide a loan for the approved total value of the project. If you change the value of the project, then the value of the loan will change also.

This sample budget is not typical as most projects end up costing more than originally intended. So a few words of caution: be very careful if you want your project to be completed within budget.

14.1 Table - Sample Budget and Actual Costs

ITEM	BUDGET	ACTUAL	TAXES	TOTAL
Land	175,000.00	174,1402.76	80.78	174,183.54
Survey	1,000.00	1,190.00	154.70	1,344.70
Printing Drawings	800.00	90.00	11.70	101.70
Building Permit	900.00	2,120.00	275.60	2436.80
Removing Trees	500.00	DIY	0.00	0.00
Mulching of Trees	1,000.00	1235.00	160.55	1,395.55
Grubbing	1,500.00	1,265.00	164.45	1,429.45
Site Services	3,000.00	2,000.00	260.00	2,260.00
Dry Well	1200.00	525.00	68.25	593.25

ITEM	BUDGET	ACTUAL	TAXES	TOTAL
Excavation	20,000.00	18,956.01	2,464.28	21,420.29
Foundation	20,000.00	15,986.00	2,078.18	18,064.18
Equipment Rentals	4,000.00	6,573.00	854.49	7,427.49
Exterior Walls	15,000.00	14,500.00	1,885.00	16,385.00
Accessories	2,000.00	1,837.38	238.86	2,076.24
Wall Concrete	6,000.00	5,686.00	739.18	6,425.18
Windows, Exterior Doors	16,000.00	12,138.51	1,578.01	13,716.52
Skylights	4,000.00	2,570.22	334.13	2,904.35
Garage Door	3,000.00	1,880.00	244.40	2,124.40
Masonry Products	6,000.00	4,418.88	574.45	4,993.33
Masonry Labour	6,000.00	4,800.00	624.00	5,424.00
Metal Flue	2,000.00	1,895.50	246.42	2,141.92
Building Supplies	20,000.00	7,394.39	961.27	8,355.66
Roof Trusses	8,000.00	6,694.99	870.35	7,565.34
Roof Decking	8,000.00	6,694.99	870.35	7,565.34
Shingles and Flashing	10,000.00	8,600.00	1,118.00	9,718.00
Dryvit	20,000.00	17,560.00	2,282.80	19,842.80
Soffits and Fascia's	4,500.00	3,250.00	422.50	3,672.50
Plumbing Fixtures	8,500.00	9,245.00	1,201.85	10,446.85
Studs and Gypsum Board	12,000.00	11,567.00	1,503.71	13,070.71
Fireplace	4,000.00	3,545.00	460.85	4,005.85
Solar Hot Water	6,600.00	6,225.00	809.25	7,034.25
Electrical	12,000.00	10,568.00	1,373.84	11,941.84
Light Fixture (allowance)	8,000.00	7,345.00	954.85	8,299.85

ITEM	BUDGET	ACTUAL	TAXES	TOTAL
Security System	3,000.00	2,235.00	290.55	2,525.55
Sound System	2,500.00	1,100.00	143.00	1,243.00
Floor Slab	15,000.00	13,458.00	1,749.54	15,207.54
Garage Slab	2,500.00	2,374.00	308.62	2,682.62
In-Floor Heating	12,000.00	10,678.00	1,388.14	12,066.14
Air to Air Heat Exchanger	6,000.00	5,375.00	698.75	6,073.75
Interior Doors and Trim	6,800.00	8,585.00	1,116.05	9,701.05
Kitchen Cabinets	15,000.00	12,373.00	1,608.49	13,981.49
Appliances	9,000.00	7,568.00	983.84	8,551.84
Painting	4,500.00	4,375.00	568.75	4,943.75
Built-ins	5,000.00	4,893.00	636.09	5,529.09
Hard Tile	10,000.00	0.00	0.00	0.00
Driveway Concrete	10,000.00	11,500.00	1,495.00	12,995.00
Walks and Patio	5,000.00	4,300.00	559.00	4,859.00
Miscellaneous	10,000.00	8,732.00	1,135.16	9,867.16
Other				
Other				
Other				
TOTAL	338,800.00	294,484.88	38,283.03	332,809.11

DIY - Do It Yourself

15. Schedule

SCHEDULING OF YOUR project is important. While it may not follow exactly as planned, a schedule will give a good indication of the length of time required to complete it. There will be things that do not go well and others that will be completed ahead of time. By having a schedule, no matter how rough it is, it will give a good indication as to when the various trades should be on-site. The subcontractors you may be hiring will have other work and your project is just another job to them so schedule their time well so that they can be there when required. While they will do what they can to meet their obligation to you, other obligations that they have can very easily disrupt all good intentions. This is not a fault; it is the nature of the business.

15.1 Table, at the end of this chapter is a sample schedule. By having your own schedule, your financial institution will be able to schedule your draws on your financing for the project. You will also be able to schedule payments to sub-contractors and building material suppliers. The sample schedule will give you an indication on the timing of each of your chosen subcontractors to be on site. It is best to start discussions with potential subcontractors early in the process. They will require final drawings and specifications to finalize their pricing for you. In the beginning they may be able to give you some "ballpark" pricing, as a start, but the drawings and specifications will be the shopping list of your actual requirements for pricing of your project. Remember, when you make changes after construction starts, the contractor's price will change. Also, depending on what stage of the project, the change occurs, if any previously constructed work that has to be removed then the costs, for the change, will increase.

If at all possible, schedule the actual construction to start during the better time of year in your region. For example, in a northern climate, assemble your drawings and specifications in the winter months and plan to start the construction in the spring and complete in the fall when the weather is usually better. This way you can also avoid the additional cost of temporary heating which will add to the overall cost of your project.

No matter how well you schedule your project, getting all the T's crossed and all the I's dotted, it will not go exactly as planned. It is the nature of the beast that you are trying to tame. But, having a schedule will help to get things back on track when you have slippage.

For example, your plumber is scheduled to arrive on Monday; the current job he is working on was delayed due to limited supply of pipe and he is trying to finish that project before he can start yours. It appears that he will be a week later getting to your project. Further, your electrician finished his last job earlier than expected and arrives a week earlier than scheduled. These are common occurrences in the construction industry and you have to be able to react positively to them, and not over-react to the detriment of the project.

There is another way to improve on your schedule. After you have finalized pricing from each of your subcontractors; ask them for their estimate of time to complete your job requirements. Also ask them what other subcontractor work needs to be completed before they can do your work without unnecessary delay. Then adjust your schedule accordingly.

Table 15.1 - SAMPLE CONSTRUCTION SCHEDULE (Page 1)

YEAR

Task Name	Duration	Start	Finish
Architectural Design	10 wks	10/14/2013	10/12/2013
Schematic Design	4 wks		
Authority Review	2 wks		
Working Drawings	4 wks		
Pre Construction	10 wks	10/12/2013	02/28/2014
Building Permit	10 wks		
Select Materials and appliances	10 wks		
Set up supplier contacts	10 wks		
CONSTRUCTION			
Mobilize	1 wks		
SITEWORK	1 wks	3/3/2014	3/10/2014
Clear Trees	1 wks		
Grub Lot	1 day		
Verify Service locations	1 day		
Temporary Toilet	1 day		
Temporary Power	1 wks		
FOUNDATIONS	3 wks	3/10/2013	3/28/2014
Excavate Footings and Walls	1 day		
Form and pour Foundation Walls	2 wks		
Insulate inside wall	1 day		
Backfill Exterior and Interior	1 day		
WALLS	6 wks	3/31/2014	5/9/2014
Erect ICF's	4 wks		
Install openings, windows,doors	1 wks		
Blockings	1 wks		
Locate required service openings	1 day		
Install re-bar	1 wks		
Pour Walls	1 day		
Strip braces	1 wks		
Place truss shoes and level	1 wks		
ROOF	5 wks	5/5/2014	6/9/2014
Erect Trusses and Rafters	2 wks		
Roof Blocking	1 wks		
Eave Framing	1 wks		
Sheathing	1 wks		
Roofing material	3 wks		
MASONRY	4 wks	6/9/2014	7/4/2014
Exterior Walls	2 wks		
Columns	1 wks		
Point joints and clean up	1 wks		
STUCCO	4 wks	7/4/2014	8/4/2014
Apply details	2 wks		
Apply coatings	2 wks		

Timeline months (weeks): March (3, 10, 17, 24, 31), April (7, 14, 21, 28), May (5, 12, 19, 26), June (2, 9, 16, 23, 30), July (7, 14, 21, 28), August (4, 11, 18, 25), September (1, 8, 15, 22, 29), October (6, 13, 20, 27), November (3, 10, 17, 24)

101

Table 15.1 - SAMPLE CONSTRUCTION SCHEDULE
(Page 2)

YEAR

Task Name	Duration	Start Date	Finish Date
FLOOR SLAB	2 wks	8/4/2014	8/18/2014
Underground Services	2 days		
Gravels	1 day		
Insulation	1 day		
Moiststop	1 day		
Welded Wire Mesh	1 day		
In Floor Heating Cables	3 days		
Pour Slab	1 day		
INTERIOR FRAMING	2 wks	8/18/2014	9/1/2014
Walls	1 wks		
Strapping	1 wks		
Ductbanks	1 wks		
Rigid and batt Insulation to Ceiling	1 wks		
ELECTRICAL & MECHANICAL	2 wks	9/1/2014	9/15/2014
Electrical Rough ins	2 wks		
Mechanical Rough ins	2 wks		
FINISHES	6 wks	9/15/2014	10/20/2014
Drywall	2 wks		
Ceilings	1 wks		
Painting	1 wks		
Kitchen Cabinets installation	1 wks		
Millwork installation	2 wks		
Kitchen Appliances	1 wks		
Specialities	1 wks		
Plumbing Fixtures	1 wks		
Light Fixtures	1 wks		
Security System	1 wks		
Sound System	1 wks		
Install Fireplace	1 wks		
EXTERIOR	2 wks	10/13/2014	10/20/2014
Concrete Paving	1 wks		
Landscaping	1 wks		
Planting	1 wks		
CLEAN UP	2 wks	10/27/2014	11/10/2014
Move furniture in	1 wks		
Final checks on systems	1 wks		

102

16. Closing

THIS BOOK HAS attempted to take you through most of the main steps it takes to build a house. These are not all as precise as you will need. You may choose to do things in a manner other than mentioned here, depending on your house design and location. Simply put, there are many ways to build a house and this book only mentions a few of the many types and processes. It is intended to give you a start for your specific project, and a logical progression through the process. You will, and should, personalize your project. Plus the construction techniques for your specific house will vary depending on your location in the world.

What follows are a few helpful hints for your project:

1. Reduce your waste as much as you can. In most areas today you cannot burn your construction waste, so you are required to truck it away to a dump site. You can have a large waste bin placed on your site and you call the providing company when it is full so that they can take it to an authorized dump site. This costs money. If you can, use as much of the wood material you have purchased for blocking, or framing, or for future kindling in your fireplace, should you have one. Return items that you have not opened or used. At least give this some thought during construction.

2. Clean up your site daily when work is done. Nothing is worse than arriving for a day of work and finding a mess in the work area. If you are not self-building then perhaps you can work an arrangement with your builder for you to keep the site clean in exchange for a credit to the contract.

3. Keep your left over paint for touch ups when they are needed. Store and label in smaller cans if need be, and keep

the correct paint numbers so the color can be re-ordered when needed. At some point the paint will dry up, most likely when you need it most, but at least you will have the number and manufacturer so it can be reordered.

4. If using brick, save several units in case some damage occurs and you may need a brick or two. Even if you have the name and manufacturer number from your original order form, the clay color can be different from the original order. Remember, the further the manufacturer goes into the clay pit for material, the more the colors will vary.

5. Save some roof shingles, or whatever material you use, in case high winds or storms cause damage and a portion is needed for repairs.

6. Save a few pieces of siding, soffit and fascia material for future reference in case a piece gets damaged. These could be stored in the truss space above the insulation - out of the way, but readily available when needed.

7. The use of local materials may keep the costs down. Also, local manufacturers are familiar with the environmental conditions in the area and their products are manufactured to respond positively to these conditions.

8. If you choose a product that may not be manufactured in the future, such as a duplex or light switch cover plates, perhaps it would be wise to have a few extra in case one gets broken, then at least you have a match to replace it. Or perhaps you take one from an area such as the garage, and replace that one with the newer model.

9. Keep a list of all the sub-contractors from your project for future reference. You never know when you may need one of them to return to your home to make a repair or add something, and who better to do the work then someone that is familiar with your home.

10. Prepare a maintenance manual. With each item you purchased for your home, literature usually comes with the package. Save that literature and put it in a three ring binder and store it in an accessible location for future reference. You can also label the sections in accordance with the titles of the chapters of this book so you can find what you want quickly. Add any other labels that may be necessary to keep this information in a proper order. When you have a problem with a particular item, you will not regret having the maintenance manual available.

11. Most communities at some time during the year will host a Home Show of new products for house construction. These are excellent opportunities to see what new products are available and to meet various people in the home construction industry. It is also an opportunity to have discussions with contractors that work the various trades in your area.

12. The internet is also a very useful tool to find information about techniques, materials and methods of construction for your particular project. It will also answer most of the technical matters that may arise during the construction of your new house.

13. Prepare a checklist with your desired outcomes, resultant outcomes and some notes for future reference in case you wish to go through the process again. Possible headings can be: Item – Desired Outcome – Resultant Outcome and Notes for possible revisions.

14. Should you decide to do some of the construction work yourself, be sure to undertake all work with the proper safety gear, such as; steel toed boots, safety gloves, safety glasses, hard hat and become familiar with all aspects of completing the work in a safe manner?

Good luck with your project.

List of Illustrations

www.ingramcontent.com/pod-product-compliance
Lightning Source LLC
Chambersburg PA
CBHW052116030426
42335CB00025B/3015